"[Vowell exercises] her trademark sweet, silly, arch sense of the incongruous ways we memorialize the American past."

—*Chicago Tribune*

"Vowell's funny, imaginative take on musty, buckled-up Pilgrim notables brings the era wickedly to life." —*The Washington Post*

"Absorbing ... [Vowell's] a complex blend: part brilliant essayist, part pop-culture-loving comedian, and a full-time unabashed history geek. The mixture makes her both proudly pointy-headed and forever entertaining. . . . Vowell's breezy style often disguises her solid craft and the richer messages below her work's shiny surface, so don't be fooled. She's a genuine treasure." —*The Seattle Times*

"Vowell's words crackle on the printed page . . . smart, quirky, and unabashedly incendiary . . . Vowell is very funny. . . . She is generous as she wrestles with the moral intricacies of our nation's beginnings and how Puritan contradictions inform our sense of American exceptionalism today. . . . *The Wordy Shipmates* is more than a punkish twist on our brave, verbose, tortured forebears, living in their new colony like 'an ashram in the woods.' Subversively, Vowell teaches as she goes, and her final reflections are genuinely moving."

—*The Cleveland Plain Dealer*

"Sarah Vowell lends her engaging voice and keen powers of observation to a work of social history. . . . [She] aims to transcend the well-worn cultural shorthand of shoe buckles and witch trials and, in doing so, provide a glimpse of what life was really like for the people of the Massachusetts Bay Colony and the founders of Plymouth."

—*Los Angeles Times*

"For those of us who'd rather harvest our history lessons from *The Simpsons* than the History Channel, Vowell is a latter-day hero. . . . Fascinating." —*Elle*

"Leave it to Sarah Vowell to unravel the most tight-laced of American archetypes: the New England Puritan. In *The Wordy Shipmates*, Vowell's latest romp through U.S. history, the wisecracking essayist and public radio personality explores a colonial culture that most people find as tough and dry as an overcooked Thanksgiving turkey. Vowell . . . [is] the kind of chatty tour guide who walks down the street backward so she can face her audience, pointing out landmarks while rattling off favorite anecdotes. . . . True to the tone of her earlier books, Vowell's writing is studded with peppy one-liners and bits of pop culture." —*The Sunday Oregonian*

"Sarah Vowell has a gift for approaching the dusty corners of Americana with a pop cultural sensibility that treats her long-dead subjects with the same mix of scrutiny and admiration that most Americans lavish on modern celebrities. . . . Vowell is so adept at breaking down the highfalutin language of the various books, letters, and pamphlets in which her subjects conducted their feuds that the impertinence and eventual banishment of colony rabble-rouser Roger Williams (who went on to found Rhode Island) reads as more dramatic than the colonies' bloody war with the Pequot nation. . . . [Her] insights into her subjects' meanings and motivations, combined with reflection and personal anecdotes—such as relating Winthrop's ideal of communal suffering and comfort to buying toothpaste for 9/11 relief workers, or an episode of *The Brady Bunch* coloring her early perceptions of the Puritans—humanize and contextualize the famously uptight settlers, reconsidering what it means for America to be called a 'Puritan nation.'" —*The A. V. Club* (*The Onion*)

"Sarah Vowell's wry explorations through history . . . combine an infectious curiosity with an uncanny ability to view solemn events through the lens of Americana camp. The end result is often a fun, gently rebellious romp through a forgotten corner of the Civil War or some other equally grave period." —*Nashville Tennessean*

"Intriguing . . . Vowell invigorates [her] subjects by imaginatively feeling her way into the conflicts and concerns of the main players in these distant dramas. She reads history with attitude, humor, and sensitivity to the texts. . . . Much of the pleasure of reading Vowell comes from her ability to connect the remote to the familiar. The difference between the orthodox Winthrop and the more tolerant, individualistic Williams, for instance, is the difference between 'Pete Seeger, gathering a generation around the campfire to sing their shared folk songs' and 'Bob Dylan plugging in at Newport, making his own noise.' We see the terms of Puritan culture playing out in more recent texts: Longfellow verses, Springsteen songs, *The Brady Bunch*. Vowell allows us to recognize the past embedded in the present—her connections are often very funny and always plausible." —*Minneapolis Star-Tribune*

"Who knew the Puritans could be so much fun? Vowell's wry wit and snarky tone make the book a lot of fun to read, but she can't hide the fact that she's moved and inspired by Winthrop's idea of America as a 'city on a hill': He calls us to be exceptional, while at the same time reminding us that we're up there as an example for all the world to see, successes and missteps alike. It's an idea as timely today as it was in 1630." —*The Wichita Eagle*

"Part scholar, part standup comic, Vowell has enlivened such dour subjects as presidential assassinations and the mistreatment of Native Americans with a mix of wisecracks, pop-culture references, and self-deprecating anecdotes." —*The Miami Herald*

"One would think it would be tough to make the topic of Pilgrims piss-pants hilarious, but the witty author-journalist nails it. . . . [A] wickedly crafted narrative . . . Vowell is . . . a comedic historian. Her topic is deeply researched, thoughtfully analyzed and, of course, diligently made fun of." —*Willamette Week* (Portland, OR)

"Vowell brings a pop-culture sensibility to the rigorous study of topics you might never think would lend themselves to it. The results are always fascinating, frequently funny, and occasionally alarming." —Authormagazine.org

"Vowell argues passionately that Puritans were as enamored of wisdom and knowledge as religious virtue. . . . Drawing on letters, essays, and sermons, Vowell offers a penetrating look at the tensions between John Winthrop, John Cotton, Roger Williams, Anne Hutchinson, and others as they argued about the role of religion in government and everyday life. . . . A book dense with detail, insight, and humor." —*Booklist* (starred review)

"Fans will be pleased to see that Vowell's admittedly smart-alecky style is alive and well: It's not every historical monograph that tosses together Anne Hutchinson and Nancy Drew, Dolly Parton and John Endecott. The author's characteristic devotion to detail is also evident . . . At times surpassingly wise." —*Kirkus Reviews*

"[A] witty exploration of the ways in which our country's present predicaments are inextricably tied to its past. . . . Gracefully interspersing her history lesson with personal anecdotes, Vowell offers reflections that are both amusing (colonial history via *The Brady Bunch*) and tender (watching New Yorkers patiently waiting in line to donate blood after 9/11)." —*Publishers Weekly* (starred review)

ALSO BY SARAH VOWELL

Lafayette in the Somewhat United States
Unfamiliar Fishes
Assassination Vacation
The Partly Cloudy Patriot
Take the Cannoli
Radio On

THE WORDY SHIPMATES

Sarah Vowell

RIVERHEAD BOOKS

New York

Riverhead Books
An imprint of Penguin Random House LLC
375 Hudson Street
New York, New York 10014

Vowell, Sarah, date.
   The wordy shipmates / Sarah Vowell.
     p. cm.
   ISBN 978-1-59448-999-0
   1. Puritans—New England—History—17th century. 2. New England—Politics and government to 1775. 3. Religion and politics—New England—History—17th century. I. Title.
F7.V69   2008   2008030491
974.088'2859—dc22

First Riverhead hardcover edition: October 2008
First Riverhead trade paperback edition: October 2009
Riverhead trade paperback ISBN: 978-1-59448-400-1

Printed in the United States of America
13   12   11   10

Cover design by Jackie Seow
Cover photograph © 2008 David Levinthal
Book design by Nicole LaRoche
Illustration by Marcel Dzama
Map by Jeffrey L. Ward

For Scott Seeley,
Ted Thompson, and Joan Kim

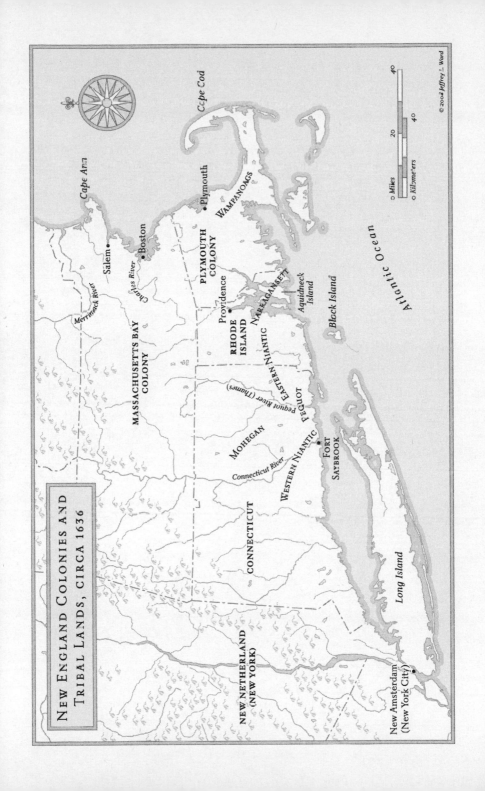

New England Colonies and Tribal Lands, circa 1636

Cape Ann

Cape Cod

Salem

Boston

Charles River

Merrimack River

PLYMOUTH COLONY

Plymouth

WAMPANOAGS

MASSACHUSETTS BAY COLONY

Providence

RHODE ISLAND

Aquidneck Island

NARRAGANSETT

EASTERN NIANTIC

Black Island

Pequot River (Thames)

PEQUOT

MOHEGAN

Connecticut River

WESTERN NIANTIC

FORT SAYBROOK

CONNECTICUT

Atlantic Ocean

Long Island

NEW NETHERLAND (NEW YORK)

New Amsterdam (New York City)

Miles

Kilometers

© 2004 Jeffrey L. Ward

But oh! shipmates! on the starboard hand of every woe, there is a sure delight. . . . Delight is to him whose strong arms yet support him, when the ship of this base treacherous world has gone down beneath him. Delight is to him, who gives no quarter in the truth, and kills, burns, and destroys all sin though he pluck it out from under the robes of Senators and Judges. Delight,—top-gallant delight is to him, who acknowledges no law or lord, but the Lord his God, and is only a patriot to heaven.

—HERMAN MELVILLE, *Moby-Dick*

The only thing more dangerous than an idea is a belief. And by dangerous I don't mean thought-provoking. I mean: might get people killed.

Take the Reverend John Cotton. In 1630, he goes down to the port of Southampton to preach a farewell sermon to the seven hundred or so colonists of the Massachusetts Bay Company. Led by Governor John Winthrop, a gentleman farmer and lawyer, these mostly Puritan dissenters are about to sail from England to New England on the flagship *Arbella* and ten other vessels in the Winthrop fleet.

By the time Cotton says amen, he has fought Mexico for Texas, bought Alaska from the Russians, and dropped napalm on Vietnam. Then he lays a wreath on Custer's grave and revs past Wounded Knee. Then he claps when the Marquis de Lafayette tells Congress that "someday America will save the world." Then he smiles when Abraham Lincoln calls the United States "the last best hope of earth." Then he frees

Cuba, which would be news to Cuba. Then he signs the lease on Guantánamo Bay.

Cotton's sermon is titled "God's Promise to His Plantation." He begins with one of the loveliest passages from the book of Second Samuel, an otherwise R-rated chronicle of King David's serial-killer years. Chapter 7, verse 10: "I will appoint a place for my people Israel, and I will plant them, that they may dwell in a place of their own, and move no more." Sounds so homey, like that column in the real estate section of the *New York Times* about how people found their apartments. Until I remember that talk like this is the match still lighting the fuses of a thousand car bombs.

What Cotton is telling these about-to-be-Americans is that they are God's new chosen people. This they like to hear. In fact, they have been telling themselves just that. The Old Testament Israelites are to the Puritans what the blues was to the Rolling Stones—a source of inspiration, a renewable resource of riffs. What Cotton is telling them is that, like the Old Testament Jews, they are men of destiny. And, like the Old Testament Jews, God has given them a new home, a promised land. And, like the Old Testament Jews, God has printed eviction notices for them to tack up on the homes of the nothing-special, just-folks folks who are squatting there.

It's fine, according to Cotton, to move into "a country not altogether void of inhabitants" if said country is really big. After all, he continues, "Abraham and Isaac, when they sojourned amongst the Philistines, they did not buy that land to feed their cattle, because they said 'There is room enough.' "

This is God's plantation, remember? Cotton says, "If God be the gardener, who shall pluck up what he sets down?" Hear that, Indians? No weeding of the white people allowed. Unless they're Catholic. Or one of those Satan-worshipping Virginians.

John Cotton is forty-six years old. He is the most respected, famous, and beloved Puritan minister in England. Getting him to bless the send-off of these relatively unimportant castaways would be like scoring Nelson Mandela to deliver the commencement address at the neighbor kid's eighth-grade graduation. In fact, once the colonists arrive in Massachusetts they will name their settlement Boston, in honor of Cotton's hometown.

These people listening to this man are scared. There's a boat in the harbor that just might sail them to their deaths. They may never see their friends again until heaven (or hell, depending on how this dumb plan goes). For years they've grumbled that England is a cesspool governed by an immoral king under the spell of the Whore of Babylon, which is their cute nickname for the pope. But now that it's time to light out, their dear old mother country seems so cozy, all warm beds and warm beer and days of *auld lang syne*.

Yet here is the smartest man in England, maybe the smartest man in the world, telling them, little old them, that they have been picked by God. They are Israelites is what they are. They are fleeing Egypt. Good riddance! Next stop, land of milk/honey.

Now they know. They can do this. They can vomit their way across the sea. They can spend ten years digging up tree stumps to plow frozen fields. They can even learn to love corn. For the first time in months, they can breathe.

Then Cotton quotes Luke 12:48. "To whom much is given, of him God will require the more." Of course there's a catch, Spider-Man. When God is the landlord, Cotton says, "defraud him not of his rent." The price? Obedience. Break God's laws and suffer ye His wrath. The Israelites, Cotton warns, "might wrong themselves by trespassing against God, and so expose themselves to affliction. . . . If Israel will destroy themselves; the fault is in themselves." Great. All this special treatment might get them nothing more than special punishment from a creator who sure is creative when it comes to retribution—the prophet swallowed by the whale, the wife turned into salt.

Thank goodness for bees. Cotton points out that when "the hive is too full, they seek abroad for new dwellings." Keep in mind that most of the colonists fear more than a watery grave, or the dark forest ahead, or even hell. They question their leaving. What if their sinful birthplace needs them? But Cotton reassures them that England has more than its fair share of Englishmen. He remarks that "when the hive of the Commonwealth is so full, that tradesmen cannot live one by another, but eat up one another in this case it is lawful to remove."

Here we arrive at the reason why this here tale of American Puritans is more concerned with the ones shipping off from Southampton for Massachusetts in the *Arbella* in 1630 than with the Pilgrims who sailed from Southampton toward Plymouth on the *Mayflower* in 1620: because the Plymouth colonists were Separatists and the Massachusetts Bay colonists were not.

Before I explain that, I will say that the theological differences between the Puritans on the *Mayflower* and the Puritans on the *Arbella* are beyond small. Try negligible to the point of nitpicky. I will also say that readers who squirm at microscopic theological differences might be unsuited to read a book about seventeenth-century Christians. Or, for that matter, a newspaper. Secular readers who marvel every morning at the death toll in the Middle East ticking ever higher due to, say, the seemingly trifling Sunni-versus-Shia rift in Islam, might look deep into their own hearts and identify their own semantic lines in the sand. For instance, a devotion to *The Godfather Part II* and equally intense disdain for *The Godfather Part III*. Someday they might find themselves at a bar and realize they are friends with a woman who can't tell any of the *Godfather* movies apart and asks if *Part II* was the one that had "that guy in the boat." Them's fightin' words, right?

Anyway, England, 1630. Question: Why is the aforementioned John Cotton standing in front of the aforementioned

John Winthrop and his shipmates, watering the seeds of American exceptionalism that will, in the twenty-first century, blossom into preemptive war in the name of spreading democracy in the Middle East that temporarily unites even some factions of the aforementioned Sunni and Shia Muslims, who hate each other's guts but agree they hate the bully America more? Answer: Because Henry VIII had a crush on a woman who was not his wife.

In order to divorce his wife, Catherine of Aragon, and marry Anne Boleyn, Henry had to divorce England from Rome. When the pope, for some reason, refused to annul the marriage vows Henry made to Catherine more than two decades earlier, Henry rebelled and established himself as the head of the Church of England in 1534. This was seventeen years after Martin Luther nailed Rome's abuses by nailing his "95 theses" to a church door in Germany, thereby welcoming in the Protestant Reformation.

Luther was outraged when the pope sent emissaries up north to raise money for St. Peter's Basilica by selling "indulgences," essentially coupons a buyer could use to pay off the pope to erase sins from the Judgment Day ledger. Luther's point was that, according to Scripture, salvation is not a bake sale: "They preach only human doctrines who say that as soon as the money clinks into the money chest, the soul flies out of purgatory." His larger message became the core ethos of Protestantism: the Bible, not any earthly pope, is the highest authority.

The word of God, not a man of God, is The Man. For that reason, Luther translated the Bible into German so Germans could read it for themselves. Which inspired various international Protestants to do the same in their own native tongues. And, in one of history's great collisions, this sixteenth-century fad for vernacular Bible translations comes about not long after Luther's countryman Johan Gutenberg had invented movable type in Europe, making it possible to print said translations on the cheap and in a hurry.

So an English subject of Henry VIII who already had a soft spot for the innovations of Luther rejoiced at the king's break with Rome (while trying not to picture Henry and Anne Boleyn doing it in every room of every castle). That is, until the Protestant sympathizer went to church and noticed that the Church of England was just the same old Catholic Church with a king in pope's clothing. Same old hierarchy of archbishop on down. Same old Latin-speaking middlemen standing between parishioners and the Bible, between parishioners and God. Same old ornamental gewgaws. Organ music! Vestments! (It is difficult to understate the Puritan abhorrence of something as seemingly trivial as a vicar's scarf.) Same old easily achieved, come-as-you-are salvation. Here's what one had to do to join the Church of England: be English. *But we want getting into heaven to be hard!* said the Puritans. *And not for everybody!*

So the English Protestants protest. One of their heroes was William Tyndale, who had exiled himself to Germany in

1524 in order to commit the crime of translating the Bible into English. Captured at Henry's request, Tyndale was strangled, then burned at the stake in 1536; his reported last words were, "Lord, open the King of England's eyes!" This prayer was answered two years later when Henry commissioned the so-called Great Bible, the first official Bible in English—based largely on the translations of, guess who, William Tyndale.

In the near century between Henry's breakup with Rome and the Massachusetts Bay colonists' departure, members of the Church of England, which is to say the English, quarreled constantly about how Protestant to become or how Catholic to remain. No surprise that the monarchs and the clergy, at the top of the cultural hierarchy, tended to be in favor of cultural hierarchy and skewed Catholic. For instance, the late King James, son of the famously Catholic Mary, Queen of Scots, threatened to "harry" the Puritans out of England.

So in Southampton, when Cotton promises the colonists that where they are going "the sons of wickedness shall afflict them no more," they know he is referring to James's son, King Charles I, and his Anglican henchmen, including the Puritans' nemesis, the Bishop of London, William Laud.

One reason Winthrop and his shipmates are hitting the road in 1630 is that Charles had dissolved the Parliament, the one check on his power, the year before. The Protestant-leaning House of Commons had passed incendiary resolutions limiting the king's powers of taxation and proclaiming the practices of "popery and Arminianism" a capital offense. Arminianism, the dogma that a believer's salvation depends merely on faith, is at odds with the Puritans' insistence that salvation is predetermined by God. Laud, a portly and haughty gentleman in a puffy robe in his National Portrait Gallery likeness, is pretty much Mr. Arminianism. It's worth remembering that, while Laud is the bogeyman in Puritan history, his more open-minded and openhearted view of how Christians get to heaven won out in Protestantism worldwide. Which is not to deny the fact that Laud was both a ruthless ogre toward the Puritans and a suck-up to Charles, delivering sermons on the divine right of kings.

(The subtext of Cotton's sermon to the voyagers is the question "Can I come, too?" Laud becomes more and more powerful and thus more threatening to Puritans. It is no co incidence that 1633, the year Laud becomes Archbishop of Canterbury, is also the year Cotton finally emigrates to Massachusetts, where he becomes Winthrop's own minister.)

Believers who wanted to "purify" the Church of England of its Catholic tendencies came to be known by the put-down "puritan." They mostly called themselves "nonconformists," or the "godly." Or, occasionally, "hot Protestants."

The more radical Puritans who severed ties to the Church of England came to be known as Separatists; they shook off all allegiance to grandiose national religion and concentrated on their own congregations, worshipping in plain, little meetinghouses. Hence the Separatists who hightailed it to Holland and then Cape Cod on the *Mayflower.* Puritans who wanted to reform the Church of England from the inside came to be known as Nonseparatists, which is to say they came to be simply unhappy. Hence, the simultaneously hopeful and guilt-ridden men and women listening to John Cotton before boarding the *Arbella,* wondering if it is right to be abandoning England at all.

I admire the *Mayflower* Pilgrims' uncompromising resolve to make a clean break, and their fortitude, so fundamental to the American national character that Sinclair Lewis called one of our core ideals "Plymouth Rock in a sleet-storm."

Still, I find the *Arbella* passengers' qualms messier and more endearing. They were leaving for the same reasons the Pilgrims left, but they had either the modesty to feel bad about it or the charitable hypocrisy to at least pretend to. Maybe it's because I live in a world crawling with separatists that I find religious zealots with a tiny bit of wishy-washy, pussy-footing compromise in them deeply attractive. Plus, half the entertainment value of watching Massachusetts Bay come to life is witnessing all the tiptoeing and deference— frequently just a pretense of deference—to the crown. Winthrop will spend most of his time as magistrate tripping all over himself to make sure King Charles doesn't get wind of any of the colony's many treasonous infractions. Because, unlike the Plymouth Separatists, the nonseparating Bostonians left England pledging to remain as English as beheadings and clotted cream.

In fact, Winthrop and six of the highest-ranking officers of the Massachusetts Bay Company sent an open letter to the king and the Church of England before their departure in 1630 titled "The Humble Request." They beseeched His Majesty and their countrymen for "their prayers, and the removal of suspicions, and misconstructions of their intentions." The Church of England is especially cajoled as "our dear mother," whom they bid adieu with "much sadness of heart and many tears in our eyes, ever acknowledging that such hope and part as we have obtained in the common salvation we have received in her bosom, and sucked it from her breasts." (Cotton will pick up on this mammary metaphor in his farewell sermon, reminding the colonists not to forget England, "the breast that gave them suck.")

"The Humble Request" is so servile it boils down to this panicky appeal: *Nothing uppity about us, Your Majesty, we're just hobos in the woods!* To hammer home the image of themselves as unthreatening and pitiable, they remind the king and his bishops that "we shall be in our poor cottages in the wilderness."

In private, however, Winthrop will soon tell his fellow colonists the very opposite. "We shall be as a city upon a hill," he says.

I n "God's Promise to His Plantation," when John Cotton tells the seafarers before him that their exodus is as natural as a bee ditching a cramped hive, it is an act of kindness, especially to John Winthrop. Not all of Winthrop's old comrades have been so quick with a *bon voyage.* When he asked his friend Robert Reyce for advice on whether or not to emigrate, Reyce sent him a churlish warning not to, starting with the fact that, at the age of forty-two, Winthrop was too damn old. "Plantations are for young men," Reyce wrote, "that can endure all pains and hunger. . . . But for one of your years to undertake so large a task is seldom seen but to miscarry." He added that the scheme would ruin Winthrop's family, and that even on the off chance his ship avoids shipwreck, he'll live across the sea on the dole, forever dependent on England "for supplies." (It must have taken all of Winthrop's considerable restraint not to ship Reyce a boatload of so-there! corn upon Boston's first harvest.) Finally, Reyce tries to dissuade Winthrop with the wilderness's shocking lack of reading material, carping, "How hard will it be for one brought up among books and learned men, to live in a barbarous place, where is no learning and less civility?"

Not so hard, it turns out. Winthrop and his shipmates and their children and their children's children just wrote their own books and pretty much kept their noses in them up until the day God created the Red Sox. One of the Puritans' descendants, Ralph Waldo Emerson of Concord, embodied the wordy tradition passed down to him when he announced, "The art of writing is the highest of those permitted to man." As the twentieth-century critic F. O. Matthiessen would complain of Emerson's bookish bent, "It can remind you of the bias of provincial New England, whose higher culture had been so exclusively one of books that it had grown incapable even of appraising the worth of other modes of expression."

The United States is often called a Puritan nation. Well, here is one way in which it emphatically is not: Puritan lives were overwhelmingly, fanatically literary. Their single-minded obsession with one book, the Bible, made words the center of their lives—not land, not money, not power, not fun. I swear on Peter Stuyvesant's peg leg that the country that became the U.S. bears a closer family resemblance to the devil-may-care merchants of New Amsterdam than it does to Boston's communitarian English majors.

History is written by the writers. The quill-crazy New Englanders left behind libraries full of statements of purpose in the form of letters, sermons, court transcripts, and diaries. Most of what we know about the history of early New England is lifted straight out of Winthrop's wonderful journal and William Bradford's also wonderful *Of Plymouth Plantation.*

The seventeenth-century Puritans are seen as the ancestors of today's anti-intellectual Protestant sects—probably because of high school productions of Arthur Miller's *The Crucible,* a fictionalization of the Salem Witch Trials of 1692, an exercise in stupidity that took place more than forty years after John Winthrop's death. In fact, today's evangelicals owe more to the Great Awakening revival movement of the

eighteenth century, in which a believer's passion and feelings came to trump book learning. Subsequent Great Awakening sequels over the next two centuries brought forth
recent innovations, including the ecstatic outbursts known
as speaking in tongues.

There wasn't any speaking in tongues going on in Massachusetts Bay, unless you count classical Greek. The Puritans
had barely nailed together their rickety cabins when they
founded Harvard so their future clergymen could receive
proper theological training in Hebrew and other biblical
languages.

The magnitude of the Puritan devotion to higher education is on display in a letter Reverend Thomas Shepard, Jr.,
wrote to his son upon the lad's admission to Harvard. (The
elder Shepard was a graduate of Harvard's class of 1653.)
The father is full of advice on how his son can be a better
student—read history for wisdom and poetry for wit, admit
when he doesn't understand something, etc. But Shepard's
note is not so much a letter to his son as a love letter to learning, expressing how he hopes the boy will approach his stud-
ies "with an appetite." He continues, "So I say to you read!
Read! Something will stick in the mind, be diligent and good
will come of it." Then he signs the letter "Pater tuus"—"your
father," in Latin.

Perry Miller, a Harvard professor who became the twentieth century's preeminent Puritan scholar, wrote:

Puritanism was not an anti-intellectual fundamentalism; it was a learned, scholarly movement that required on the part of the leaders, and as much as possible from the followers, not only knowledge but a respect for the cultural heritage. Being good classicists, they read Latin and Greek poetry, and tried their hands at composing verses of their own. The amount they wrote, even amid the labor of settling a wilderness, is astonishing.

One of the Puritans' descendants, future president John Adams, studied at Harvard under Professor John Winthrop, our Winthrop's great-great-grandson. Writing the constitution for the Commonwealth of Massachusetts in 1778, Adams included a paragraph entitled "The Encouragement of Literature, Etc.," which, his recent biographer David McCullough points out, "was like no other declaration to be found in any constitution ever written until then, or since." It reads:

Wisdom and knowledge, as well as virtue, diffused generally among the body of the people being necessary for the preservation of their rights and liberties; and as these depend on spreading the opportunities and advantages of education in various parts of the country, and among the different orders of the people, it shall be the duty of legislators and magistrates in all future periods of this commonwealth to cherish the interests of literature and the sciences, and all seminaries of them, especially the university at Cambridge, public schools, and grammar schools in the towns; to encourage private societies and public institutions, rewards and immunities, for the promotion of agriculture, arts, sciences, commerce, trades, manufactures, and a natural history of the country; to countenance and inculcate the principles of humanity and general benevolence, public and private charity, industry and frugality, honesty and punctuality in their dealings, sincerity, good humor, and all social affections, and generous sentiments among the people.

"It was, in all," writes McCullough, "a declaration of Adams's faith in education as the bulwark of the good society, the old abiding faith of his Puritan forebears." Compare that lovely insight to the typical Puritan spoilsport cartoon.

Like any other American educated in public schools, my youthful encounters with New England colonials focused on Plymouth in 1620 and Salem in 1692. Which is to say that I read *The Crucible* in eleventh grade and I participated in elementary school Thanksgiving pageants in which children wearing construction-paper Pilgrim hats linked arms with others wearing Indian costumes consisting entirely of gift-shop souvenir Sioux headdresses and sang "God Bless America" and "This land was made for you and me."

But really, as a child I learned almost everything I knew about American history in general and British colonials in particular from watching television situation comedies. The first time I realized this, I was attending a wedding in London. A friend of the groom's, an English novelist, cornered my American friend and me and asked us to name the British general from the Revolutionary War whom Americans hate the most. He needed one of the American characters in the novel he was working on to mention in passing our most loathed Redcoat foe.

"Um, maybe Cornwallis?" I said, adding that we don't really know the names of any of the British except for the American traitor Benedict Arnold.

When the novelist asked why that was, my friend answered, "Because *The Brady Bunch* did an episode about him. Peter Brady had to play Benedict Arnold in a school play."

True, I thought. The Bradys also taught us that the Robin Hood–like Jesse James was actually a serial killer; that the ancient indigenous religious culture of the Hawaiian Islands is not to be messed with; and that the Plymouth Pilgrims had a bleak first winter that was almost as treacherous to live through as that time Marcia got bonked in the face with her brothers' football and her nose swelled up right before a big date.

In fact, the *Brady Bunch* Puritan episode is an educational twofer. Because its premise involves Greg Brady shooting a movie about the *Mayflower* Pilgrims using his family as actors, the viewer can learn about the hardships of colonial New England while at the same time learning about the hardships of directing an independent film. Greg's parents and the housekeeper, Alice, give too many notes on his screenplay. His brothers only want to play Indians, and all three of his bickering sisters demand to play the role of the Puritan girl Priscilla Alden. So Greg lets loose a tirade about artistic vision. He yells, "I want to write my own screenplay, design my own sets, choose my costumes, and pick the actors. Don't you see it's my project?"

Greg's final product is full of factual holes—like the off-hand remark alluding to the so-called first Thanksgiving that "the Pilgrims made friends with the Indians and invited them to a feast," when it was actually the Indians who taught the agriculturally challenged Englishmen how to plant corn in the first place. But there is one interesting exchange that's a pretty accurate picture of a child coming to terms with American history.

Bobby and Peter, who have agreed to play Pilgrims in some scenes and Indians in others, are dressed up in kitschy Plains Indian–type garb. When Greg asks them if they know what to do, Peter answers, "Yeah, attack the fort." When Greg and their mother point out that these are friendly Indians, so there won't be an attack, Bobby asks, "Then what do you need Indians for?"

"Bobby, the Indians were friendly at first," says Mr. Brady. "They didn't start fighting until their land was taken away."

Bobby: "You mean the Pilgrims took away all the Indians' land?"

"That's right," answers Mr Brady, who immediately looks regretful at this point-blank lapse of patriotic-forefather boosterism and adds, "Uh, well, at first they didn't take much of it."

"Then how about not much of an attack?" cracks Peter. And that's the end of the original sin question. After all, they have bigger logistical headaches at hand, like creating a realistic snowstorm using a box of breakfast cereal operated by one of the decidedly nonunion kid brothers.

From *Mr. Ed* to *The Simpsons,* there are actually a surprising number of sitcoms that have done episodes set in seventeenth-century New England. Even though seventeenth-century New England is all situation and no comedy.

I was in third grade when I saw the *Happy Days* Thanksgiving episode. The whole cast was in Puritan garb. Joanie Cunningham complains that "being a Pilgrim sure is a draggeth." The Fonz says things like "Greetethamundo." Here is the moment that inspired the first epiphany I ever had about colonial New England: Joanie leaves the room and her goody-goody brother Richie asks, "Father, are you letting her go out like that? Have you seen her skirt? It's up to her ankles!" I remember sitting there watching that and realizing, for the first of many times, "*Oh.* Maybe the people who founded this country were kind of crazy."

Later in the episode it is revealed that the person who

gave us Thanksgiving was not Squanto or Plymouth governor William Bradford but rather the Fonz. All the Pilgrims
were afraid of the Indians except Pilgrim Fonzie, who was
their friend. Then Joanie gets her foot caught in one of Potsy's stupid beaver traps. (That Potsy.) Remember that thing
Fonzie does with the jukebox? Where he whacks it with his
fist and the music plays? Turns out that works on beaver
traps, too. They open right up. But he won't free Joanie until
everyone renounces their racism and acts nice to the Indians and invites them to dinner. Fonzie? He's the Martin Luther King of candied yams.

Mostly, sitcom Puritans are rendered in the tone I like to
call the *Boy, people used to be so stupid* school of history. *Bewitched* produced not one but two time-travel witch trial episodes—one for each Darrin. They're both diatribes about
tolerance straight out of *The Crucible,* but with cornier dia-
logue and magical nose crinkles. The housewife/witch
Samantha brings a ballpoint pen with her to seventeenth-
century Salem and the townspeople think it's an instrument
of black magic. So they try her for witchcraft and want to
hang her.

Check out those barbarian idiots with their cockamamie
farce of a legal system, locking people up for fishy reasons
and putting their criminals to death. Good thing Americans
put an end to all that nonsense long ago.

My point being, the amateur historian's next stop after
Boy, people used to be so stupid is *People: still stupid.* I could

look at that realization as a woeful lack of human progress.
But I choose to find it reassuring. Watching *Bewitched* and
The Brady Bunch again, I was flummoxed as to why they
made such a big deal about *Mayflower* voyagers John and
Priscilla Alden. Then I figured out that those two once
loomed so large in the American mind mostly because
schoolchildren used to spend every November reading
Henry Wadsworth Longfellow's 1858 love-triangle poem
about the Aldens called "The Courtship of Miles Standish."
The poem is full of all kinds of hooey, like calling Alden a
scholar, even though in real life he was the guy on the *Mayflower* the Pilgrims hired as their barrel maker. Basically, he
was in charge of the beer. And we should expect nothing less
from Longfellow, who also poetically pumped up the importance of Paul Revere. There isn't that much difference between tall tales that start "Listen, my children, and you shall
hear" and "Here's the story of a man named Brady." In other
words, Americans have learned our history from exaggerated
popular art for as long as anyone can remember. Revolutionary War soldiers were probably singing fun but inaccurate
folk songs about those silly Puritans to warm themselves by
the fire at Valley Forge. Right before they defeated that godforsaken General Cornwallis, of course. Man, I hate that guy.

A search through a sampling of American newspapers
from the last few weeks for the word "Puritan" yields

the following. An article on how much baby boomers are looking forward to retirement because they've always rolled their eyes at the "Puritan work ethic" since their turn on/drop out youths and thus can't wait to spend their golden years traveling, volunteering, playing golf, and farming—the article really did say farming, which, I hate to break it to the flower children, is a pretty hard job. A financial analyst, speaking of a recent crackdown on mortgage lending, opines, "The transition from drunken sailor to being a Puritan was awfully fast." A profile of painter turned filmmaker Julian Schnabel claims "Puritan critics" always looked down on the artist's charismatic joie de vivre. A sports columnist waxes happily that the national ardor for athletic events holds together our otherwise "fragmented society" in spite of "our Puritan forefathers' deep distrust of any kind of play."

I'm always disappointed when I see the word "Puritan" tossed around as shorthand for a bunch of generic, boring, stupid, judgmental killjoys. Because to me, they are very specific, fascinating, sometimes brilliant, judgmental killjoys who rarely agreed on anything except that Catholics are going to hell.

Certainly the Puritans believed and said and did many unreasonable things. That kind of goes with the territory of being born before the Age of Reason. Ponder all the cockamamie notions we moderns have been spared simply by coming into this world after an apple conked Sir Isaac Newton in the head.

The Puritans' yearning for knowledge, especially their establishment of a college so early on, was self-correcting. In fact, it is Puritan father John Winthrop's great-great-grandson, the Harvard scientist who taught John Adams, who would be nicknamed the father of seismology. (After an earthquake shook Boston in 1755 and prompted the usual religious flipouts about the wrath of God, Professor Winthrop delivered an influential lecture at Harvard proposing the earthquake might have been caused by heat and pressure below the surface of the earth. With God's help, of course, but God comes off as an engineer instead of a hothead vigilante.)

This book is about those Puritans who fall between the cracks of 1620 Plymouth and 1692 Salem, the ones who settled the Massachusetts Bay Colony and then Rhode Island during what came to be called the Great Migration. (Between 1629, when King Charles I dissolves the Puritan-friendly English Parliament, and 1640, when the English Civil War begins and the Puritans under Oliver Cromwell eventually behead Charles and run the country, more than 20,000 English men, women, and children settled in New England.)

I am concentrating primarily on the words written or spoken during the Great Migration era by the Puritans of the Massachusetts Bay Colony (mostly John Winthrop and John Cotton) and those of two exiles, Roger Williams and Anne Hutchinson, who went on to found settlements in Rhode Island after Winthrop and his fellow magistrates kicked them out of Massachusetts. Because, despite the gallingly voluminous quantity of their scribblings and the court records of their squabbles, nowadays the founders of New England are more or less mute.

Most college-educated American citizens can cough up a line or two from the Founding Fathers and Abraham Lincoln. However, among my friends who are fortyish or younger, the only direct quote from seventeenth-century Massachusetts I could get was from my friend Daniel. He knows that when Salem's Giles Corey refused to testify when accused of witchcraft, the magistrates piled rocks on top of his body to try and persuade him, until he was pressed to death. What Corey said to his tormentors—"More weight!"— is Daniel's name for his computer's hard drive.

The most important reason I am concentrating on Winthrop and his shipmates in the 1630s is that the country I live in is haunted by the Puritans' vision of themselves as God's chosen people, as a beacon of righteousness that all others are to admire. The most obvious and influential example of that mind-set is John Winthrop's sermon "A Model of Christian Charity," in which he calls on New England to be "as a city upon a hill." The most ironic and entertaining example of that mind-set is the Massachusetts Bay Colony's official seal. The seal, which the Winthrop fleet brought with them from England, pictures an Indian in a loincloth holding a bow in one hand and an arrow in the other. Words are coming out of his mouth. The Indian says, "Come over and help us."

That is really what it says.

The worldview behind that motto —we're here to help, whether you want our help or not—is the Massachusetts Puritans' most enduring bequest to the future United States. And like everything the Puritans believed, it is derived from Scripture. In Acts, chapter 16, one night the Apostle Paul has a vision. In the vision, a Macedonian man appears and tells him, "Come over into Macedonia, and help us." So Paul heads west.

So westward sails the *Arbella* in 1630. And then one night almost three centuries later President William McKinley will pray to God and God will tell him to help the Filipinos by Christianizing them (even though they have been Catholics for two hundred years), "and the next morning," he says, "I sent for the chief engineer of the War Department (our mapmaker) and told him to put the Philippines on the map of the United States." So westward sail the gunboats toward Manila Bay. And then in the 1960s, President John F. Kennedy, believing that the United States must "bear the burden . . . of helping freedom defend itself," invades Vietnam; otherwise, he explains, "if we stop helping them, they will become ripe for internal subversion and a Communist takeover." So westward sail the aircraft carriers toward Saigon Harbor. And then, because the U.S. will keep on going west to help people until we're going east, the warships and the F-117 stealth fighters hurry toward the Persian Gulf. On

March 19, 2003, President George W. Bush announced that "American and coalition forces are in the early stages of military operations to disarm Iraq, to free its people and to defend the world from grave danger." Five days earlier, Vice President Dick Cheney appeared on *Meet the Press* and his words redrew the seal of the Massachusetts Bay Colony, replacing the Indian with a citizen of Baghdad, begging, "Come over and help us." Of the American invasion, Cheney claimed, "My belief is that we will, in fact, be greeted as liberators." After all, we're there to help.

In the present-day United States, the Massachusetts Puritans' laughable, naïve, and self-aggrandizing idea that they were leaving England partly to come over and help American Indians who were simply begging for their assistance has won out over the Founding Fathers' philosophy of not firing shots in other countries' wars. In his 1801 inaugural address, Thomas Jefferson argued for "peace, commerce, and honest friendship with all nations—entangling alliances with none."

During the 2008 presidential primaries, the one candidate who brought up that Jefferson quote was outsider Congressman Ron Paul, who equated being in favor of the war in Iraq with disagreeing with the Founders. "Since so many apparently now believe Washington and Jefferson were wrong on the critical matter of foreign policy," he said, "they should at least have the intellectual honesty to admit it." This sort of talk did not endear Paul to Republican primary voters.

L et's return to the coast of England in 1630 as John Cotton preaches to the Winthrop fleet. Cotton would have been aware of the pros-and-cons list Winthrop and his fellows in the Massachusetts Bay Company wrote and passed around among the godly, enumerating the reasons to go to America. In the various similar versions of this tract, Winthrop and Co. are trying to talk themselves and other potential colonists into going; but just as importantly, they're also trying to justify the venture to loved ones they're leaving behind, the family and friends who have a right to feel hurt if not downright insulted by this abandonment.

Two things especially weigh on Winthrop and his shipmates —news from Europe and news at home. Over the previous dozen years, continental Catholics and Protestants had been killing each other relentlessly, from Sweden to Spain, from France to Bohemia, in what came to be known as the Thirty Years' War. (As much as a fifth of the population of what would become Germany died.) The English couldn't help but worry the war would spread across the Channel. As Thomas Hooker would preach not long after the *Arbella* sailed:

Will you have England destroyed? Will you put the aged to trouble, and your young men to the sword? Will you have your young women widows, and your virgins defiled? Will you have your dear and tender little ones tossed upon the pikes and dashed upon the stones? Or will you have them brought up in Popery . . . perishing their souls forever, which is worst of all? . . . Will you see England laid waste without inhabitants?

After Charles I dissolved Parliament in 1629, Winthrop became convinced England was courting the wrath of God. He wrote a letter to his wife, Margaret, confessing that he feared that since God had already made the European Protestants "drink of the bitter cup of tribulation," the unrepentant English would surely be served "the very dregs." He continued, "God will bring some heavy affliction upon this land, and that speedily." And so, he told Margaret about escaping to America, "If the Lord sees it will be good for us, he will provide a shelter and a hiding place for us and others."

The tract about the pros and cons of emigration that Winthrop wrote, most likely together with the Puritan ministers John White and Francis Higginson, was given the catchy title *Reasons to Be Considered for Justifying the Undertakers of the Intended Plantation in New England, and for Encouraging Such Whose Hearts God Shall Move to Join with Them in It.* It is a handy, albeit touchy, account of the Massachusetts Bay Company's objectives in the New World, and objections to the Old. Clearly, they believe England is in trouble, if not doomed. "The departing of good people from a country does not cause a judgment," they write, "but warns of it."

Again, Hooker, who would echo this run for-your-lives sentiment before taking off for America via Holland:

> So glory is departed from England; for England hath seen her best days, and the reward of sin is coming on apace; for God is packing up of his gospel, because none will buy his wares. . . . God begins to ship away his Noahs, which prophesied and foretold that destruction was near; and God makes account that New England shall be a refuge for his Noahs and his Lots, a rock and a shelter for his righteous ones to run unto; and those that were vexed to see the ungodly lives of the people in this wicked land, shall there be safe.

Honestly, I wish I weren't so moved by this Puritan quandary. I wish I did not identify with their essential questions: What if my country is destroying itself? Could I leave? Should I? And if so, what time's the next train to Montreal?

Well, maybe not Montreal. The first reason Winthrop's pros-and-cons tract gives for crossing the Atlantic is to build a Protestant New England as an antidote to Catholic New France, to "raise a bulwark against the kingdom of Antichrist, which the Jesuits labor to rear up in those parts." Antichrist, by the way, is another name they call the pope.

Their other arguments for getting gone? Overpopulation ("England grows weary of her inhabitants"); the universities at Oxford and Cambridge are "corrupted" and "ruffianlike" and cost too much; God gave the Indians land and they aren't really using it (no cattle); the Indians can "learn from us" about God (and, presumably, cattle); they will avoid hard times like the recent drought in Virginia (known as "the starving time") because, unlike the Virginians, they are nei-ther "sloth" nor "scum"; and, regarding Massachusetts, "God hath consumed the natives with a great plague in those parts, so as there be few inhabitants left."

I take back what I said about how there's nothing more dangerous than a belief. Sometimes there's nothing more dangerous than a germ.

"From 1492 to 1650, contagions claimed as many as nine [native] lives out of ten. . . . The kingdom of death extended from Chile to Newfoundland." I saw those words printed next to a map of North and South America when I visited the Smithsonian's National Museum of the American Indian. The map is black and white but it has a red light on a timer inside, so the Americas turn bloodier and bloodier all day long, like some kind of lava lamp of loss.

Standing in front of that map I let those numbers sink in. Nine out of ten. I learned to count by singing that old min-strel song turned nursery rhyme, "Ten Little Indians." Now I have that melody stuck in my head and I'm picturing seven little, eight little, nine little Aztecs struck dead by smallpox.

I guess I knew all this. But watching the map blush so many times, I'm dizzy, so dizzy I have to look for a chair. And once I sit in the chair I feel like I'm learning to count all over again.

Ninety percent.

Way before Europeans started building settlements in the Americas and intentionally killing natives, thanks to the earliest European ramblers—the explorers, the fishermen, and other pale-faced entrepreneurs and rubbernecks passing through—European microorganisms moved here for good right away.

Just before the Pilgrims set foot in Plymouth in 1620, the plague of 1616–19 that Winthrop and the others reference in their tract wiped out New England tribes. Remember Squanto, the legendary English-speaking Indian, hero of the First Thanksgiving? He spoke English because he had learned it in Europe after he was kidnapped by sailors. By the time he made his way back to America, everyone he knew was dead. Plymouth was actually built on the site of Squanto's hometown, Patuxet. All his friends and family, his whole village, were killed off by the diseases that arrived with earlier European visitors. Squanto was hanging around Plymouth because it was the only home he knew. That's why he was there to help the incompetent white people grow corn—using seeds they'd stolen from some other Indians on Cape Cod.

When King James learned of the epidemic he thanked "Almighty God in his great goodness and bounty toward us" for "this wonderful plague among the savages."

It wasn't only the insufferable James, whom Winston Churchill described as having assumed the crown "with a closed mind, and a weakness for lecturing," who made such unkind remarks. Winthrop saw the plague the same way. "God hath thereby cleared our title to this place," he wrote.

Even the nineteenth-century abolitionist (and Puritan descendant) Harriet Beecher Stowe, author of *Uncle Tom's Cabin,* had a moral blind spot where the continent's original inhabitants were concerned. According to her son and grandson, upon reading as a child that "a plague had wasted the Indian tribes, and so prepared a place for the Pilgrim fathers to settle undisturbed" she felt "that the very ground under her feet was consecrated by some special dealings of God's wonder-working providence."

An excerpt from Anglo adventurer Thomas Morton's *New English Canaan* is printed next to the kingdom of death map in the museum. Describing his first trip to New England in 1622, he writes that the Indians "died in heaps as they lay in their houses. . . . And the bones and skulls upon the several places of their habitations made such a spectacle . . . that, as I traveled in that forest near Massachusetts it seemed to me a new Golgotha." Golgotha, the museum points out, means "place of the skull."

Next to Morton's grim account is this one from *The De Soto Chronicles* of 1540 about how disease had turned parts of the American Southeast into a wasteland: "About this place . . . were large vacant towns grown up in grass that appeared as if no people had lived in them for a long time."

When I was reading up on the plague, one sentence in James W. Loewen's *Lies My Teacher Told Me* startled me. Loewen writes that "after a smallpox epidemic the Cherokee," according to anthropologist William S. Willis, " 'despaired so much that they lost confidence in their gods and the priests destroyed the sacred objects of the tribe.' "

I was born in eastern Oklahoma and both my parents have Cherokee ancestors who were forced west on the Trail of Tears in 1838. I have in my possession two family heirlooms—a crumbling copy of *The Constitution and Laws of the Cherokee Nation,* published in 1875, and my great-grandmother's high school diploma from the Cherokee Female Seminary (the first school for girls west of the Mississippi), dated 1898. These are probably the two items I own that I would reach for as I sprinted for the door in case of fire. But they are exceedingly Cherokee artifacts, which is to say they are embarrassingly English: a law book pretty much straight from the quill of James Madison, and a young lady's diploma from Bible school. Of the so-called Five Civilized Tribes of the Southeast, the Cherokee, even when I was young, still prided themselves on being the most civilized of all—the most Christian, the best behaved, the only North American tribe with an alphabet, invented by Sequoyah in 1821. And I have always been a little uneasy about what seems like a striving for whiteness. It's just ever so craven.

I'm a tad Seminole, too. Now there's a tribe with backbone. Swamp fights! Osceola stabbing Andrew Jackson's treaty with a knife! Technically, the Seminole are, to this day, still at war with the United States.

So I always cringed, wondering why, when the English showed up, most of the Cherokee dropped whatever they were doing and adopted English ways on the spot, from becoming Christians and speaking English to eventually printing their own newspaper, ratifying a constitution, and owning black slaves like the white Southerners they aspired to be. Perhaps this is why: they "despaired so much that they lost confidence in their gods and the priests destroyed the sacred objects of the tribe." It makes so much sense. Some microscopic predator comes along and wipes out most of the tribe and *of course* they would abandon their gods. Their gods abandoned them. Of course, they would take one look at the English—so alive, so well—and bow down to this English deity with so much mojo he endows his believers with some magical vaccine. I'm starting to see my family heirlooms not just as artifacts of American history but rather artifacts in the history of immunology.

The following words are written next to that bloody map of the Americas in the National Museum of the American Indian: "That initial explosion of death is one of the greatest tragedies in human history because it was unintended and unavoidable, and even inevitable. But what happened in its wake was not."

John Winthrop's sermon "A Model of Christian Charity" would not be published until 1838, 208 years after it was written. That was the year Liliuokalani, the last queen of Hawaii, was born in Honolulu; by century's end, she would be ousted in a coup d'état by the white sons of New England missionaries; eventually, her kingdom became the fiftieth of the fifty states. Eighteen thirty-eight was also the year my Cherokee great-something grandparents were trudging west at gunpoint so the white citizens of Georgia, the Carolinas, and Tennessee could take their land.

Thus Winthrop's lay sermon, with its now famous proposal that Massachusetts should be "as a city upon a hill," resurfaced just in time for John L. Sullivan to declare that the United States had a right to "the whole of Oregon" because it is America's "manifest destiny to overspread and to possess the whole of the continent which Providence has given us for the development of the great experiment of liberty and federated self-government entrusted to us."

Entrusted by whom? By God. The same "God Almighty in His most holy and wise providence" Winthrop praises for sailing the *Arbella* to New England.

Legend has it Winthrop wrote and delivered "A Model of Christian Charity" on the *Arbella* in the middle of the Atlantic in 1630. Some scholars now contend he wrote it in England and delivered it back in Southampton before shoving off, perhaps on the very same occasion as Cotton preached his farewell sermon, "God's Promise to His Plantation." If that Winthrop-Cotton double bill is true, the only thing that would make the program a more exceptional event in the history of American exceptionalism is if Theodore Roosevelt showed up to conduct a brassy version of "America the Beautiful" performed by the United States Marine Corps Band.

Wherever Winthrop wrote or delivered "Christian Charity," it is up for debate. This isn't: at the time, nobody cared. Winthrop's biographer, Francis J. Bremer, notes that

> not a single individual recorded in letter, diary, or other source having heard Winthrop deliver the sermon. The only contemporary reference to the sermon that survives is the Reverend Henry Jessey's request that John Winthrop Jr. send him copies of a number of papers relating to the colony, including "the Model of Charity." Whereas Cotton's farewell was published soon after it was delivered, "Christian Charity" was not. Indeed, only one contemporary manuscript copy of Winthrop's work survives, and it is not in his handwriting.

When Bremer says the sermon is not mentioned in any diary, he is including Winthrop's own journal. No *I killed with my charity bit on the Lido Deck tonight* to be found.

Bremer and others contend that Winthrop's sermon didn't make much of a splash at the time because the governor wasn't saying anything the average Puritan hadn't heard in many a fortnight.

Reading Cotton's "God's Promise to His Plantation" alone hints that dissenting English Protestants had plenty of we're-God's-special-chosen-people talk to go around. So maybe Winthrop co-opting the image of a city on a hill from the Gospel of Matthew was just one more metaphor for the pile. Maybe that was the hill the city would be built on—a teetering stack of self-congratulatory biblical comparisons.

"Christian Charity" begins: "God Almighty in His most holy and wise providence, hath so disposed of the condition of mankind, as in all times some must be rich, some poor, some high and eminent in power and dignity; others mean and in subjection."

Winthrop couldn't know that overturning what he just said would become the definition of the American dream. Compare his hard, cold fact that "some must be rich, some poor" to the shocking second sentence of the Declaration of Independence, written 146 years later: "We hold these truths to be self-evident, that all men are created equal, that they are endowed by their Creator with certain unalienable Rights, that among these are Life, Liberty and the pursuit of Happiness." By 1776, the Creator seems to have learned to delegate some of His authority to His creations.

In 1630, however, the truth that all men are created equal is far from self-evident. Winthrop is saying the opposite— that God created all men unequal. To Winthrop, this is a good thing, especially since he's in charge. The beauty of this inequity, he claims, is "that every man might have need of others, and from hence they might be all knit more nearly together in the bonds of brotherly affection." To a modern reader, this social theory smacks of "I need you to mow my lawn and you need me not to report you to Immigration." But to Winthrop, the societal food chain is more sentimental. More than anything, "A Model of Christian Charity" is a declaration of *de*pendence.

One of his shipmates on the *Arbella*, budding poet Anne Bradstreet, would echo Winthrop's sentiment later on to the extent that it might be proof that someone on the boat actually heard him. She wrote, "As it is with countries, so it is with men: there was never yet any one man that had all excellences," and so "he stands in need of something which another man hath. . . . God will have us beholden one to another."

Because of the "city upon a hill" sound bite, "A Model of Christian Charity" is one of the formative documents outlining the idea of America. But dig deep into its communitarian ethos and it reads more like an America that might have been, an America fervently devoted to the quaint goals of working together and getting along. Of course, this America does exist. It's called Canada.

Every settler on the Winthrop fleet automatically became more important, more necessary, just by leaving England. That is true for Winthrop most of all. In Massachusetts, he will be governor—the highest authority in the land. In England, he is at best a middling sort—an average member of the landowning gentry. He is a justice of the peace in his run-of-the-mill county in East Anglia; he keeps having to divvy up amongst his sons the estate his father acquired from Henry VIII after Henry booted all the Catholic monks from their monasteries; he travels frequently to London for his job as a workaday real estate attorney at the king's court; he is only friends with Members of Parliament, not a member himself, and if he had ambitions to become an MP, they were surely dashed when Charles I scrapped Parliament altogether.

Winthrop's friends in the Massachusetts Bay Company were shrewd talent scouts who saw something in Winthrop, some potential greatness, and recruited him to emigrate and become their CEO. Winthrop sees the faith of his peers as a revelation of God's calling. It is, to him, a promotion. And not just an upgrade in social status. The governorship is an opportunity to better serve God. "When a man is to wade through a deep water," wrote Winthrop when he was mulling over the move, "there is required tallness."

This contradiction—between humility before God and the egomania unleashed by being chosen by God—is true of both Winthrop and the colony of Massachusetts itself. This man hopes for tallness for himself as well as for his future city, pitched, in his mind, above sea level, on yonder hill.

It is no accident that Winthrop speaks of "God Almighty in His most holy and wise providence" at the sermon's start. The English Puritans were obsessed with the idea of providence, and that word is more ominous to them than it sounds to us. It means care, but it also means control. It does not just mean that God will provide. It means that God will provide whatever the hell God wants and the Puritans will thank Him for it even if He provides them with nothing more than a slow death in a long winter. It means that if they're scared and small and lowly enough He just might toss a half-eaten corncob their way. It means that the world isn't fair and it's their fault. It means that God is the sovereign, the *authority*. It means manna from heaven, but it also means bow down.

The Puritans live and worship within a specific subset of the Protestant Reformation—Calvinism. After Mary Tudor assumed the English throne in 1553, she reinstated Catholicism as the state religion and persecuted Protestants. For this the queen acquired the nickname "Bloody Mary." To avoid being burned at the stake, many English Protestants fled to Europe, especially to John Calvin's church in Geneva. There, a committee of them wrote, edited, and revised a new version of the Bible in English, published in 1560. Its margins were annotated with especially Protestant interpretations of Scripture. For example, the note to Revelation 11:7 claims that the beast in the bottomless pit mentioned in the verse is "the Pope, which hath his power out of hell." Or the note on Revelation 17, which claims that the woman wearing scarlet riding a scarlet beast is "the Antichrist, that is, the Pope, with the whole body of his filthy creatures."

The Geneva Bible was in fact the inspiration for the King

James Bible, the version authorized by that monarch in 1611. James was infuriated by the notes in the Geneva Bible because he thought they undermined belief in the divine right of kings. He especially hated the note in the first chapter of Exodus, in which Hebrew midwives defied the king's mandate to kill all male Hebrew babies. The Geneva note claimed that the midwives' "disobedience was lawful."

Even though the King James Version was available to them, the Geneva Bible is the one the Calvinists on the *Mayflower* and most travelers in the Winthrop fleet carried with them to America.

Winthrop and his fellow Calvinists believed in the doctrine of predestination. Since God decides everything, God decides whether a person will end up in heaven or hell before the person is even born. The people who are going to heaven are called "the Elect." This is God's own aristocracy. And if that sounds like some frolicsome foxhunt, understand that to be a Calvinist is to be the Duke of Discomfort or the Duchess of Fear. Because here's the thing: How does anyone *know*? How does anyone know if he's saved? He can't. What he can do is work, try, believe, repent, love God, and hate himself. The diligent, hardworking, and pious are the "visible saints." If a person *seems* saved, odds are he is saved. Thus, he will spend every waking hour trying to seem saved, not just to others but to himself. Because if he says or does or even thinks heretical things, isn't that just proof he was never saved in the first place?

Let's hazard a guess that some people are not going to be up for this. The constant uncertainty—is it streets of gold for me or am I merely lighter fluid for the flames of hell?—weighs on the believer. Even John Calvin himself, the French theologian who popularized this school of thought, wrote the following in his last will and testament:

> The will I have had, and the zeal, if it can be called that, have been so cold and sluggish that I feel deficient in everything and everywhere. . . . Truly, even the grace of forgiveness [God] has given me only renders me all the more guilty, so that my only recourse can be this, that being the father of mercy, he will show himself the father of so miserable a sinner.

So if John Calvin doubts he's a good enough Calvinist—which is of course the most Calvinist thought he could have—imagine the jangling nerves of John Q. Puritan. In his journal, Winthrop writes the following about an acquaintance who was driven mad by spiritual doubt and took action to decide her fate once and for all:

> A woman of Boston congregation, having been in much trouble of mind about her spiritual estate, at length grew into utter desperation, and could not endure to hear of any comfort, etc., so as one day she took her little infant and threw it into a well, and then came into the house

and said, now she was sure she should be damned, for she
had drowned her child.

That's how heavy the weight of Calvinism can be—that a
mother would seek relief in murdering her own offspring.

But for John Winthrop and the men and women like him,
this way of life is a stirring challenge, a thrilling project, and
sometimes even a joy. Tallness! Get up early! So much to do!
Never bored! Reflect! Overthink! Repent!

In his sermon "A True Sight of Sin" Thomas Hooker rev-
els in the effort of self-examination. A half-hearted Christian
sits in a comfortable chair and peruses his own sins "by his
fireside and happily reads the story of these in a book." A
true Calvinist, on the other hand, is a kind of war correspon-
dent on the move, one who has "passed through many countries" of "barrenness and meanness" and witnessed "ruin and
desolation." By going to the trouble of taking a hard look at his
own crimes against God, the Calvinist knows "what sin is and
what it hath done, how it hath made havoc of his peace . . . and
made him a terror to himself." Which, to these people, is a
good thing. This is the terror that keeps the sinner awake to
his own shortcomings. And with fear comes adrenaline.

In the spiritual diary Winthrop started keeping in 1606,
he wrote a pious to do list on May 23, 1613. He was twenty-
six. He pledges to God that he will "carefully avoid vain and
needless expenses." He promises to "diligently observe the
Lord's Sabbath." To try and keep his mornings "free for pri-

vate prayer, meditation and reading." He "will flee idleness and much worldly business." He "will often pray . . . with my wife."

The first time I read that I wondered where I had seen it before. Then I realized it was at the end of *The Great Gatsby,* the great novel of ambition. After the striving title character meets his tragic end, his father arrives from Minnesota for the funeral, bringing with him a book in which his son had inscribed a list of his ambitions as a youth. There is a rigid schedule that begins with getting up early, and filling the day with work, exercise, and study. From five until six p.m., he is to "Practice elocution, poise and how to attain it." Then, in a list of "general resolves," he orders himself to quit smoking and wasting time, "read one improving book or magazine per week," set money aside, and "be better to parents." Gatsby's father tells Gatsby's friend the list proves that his boy "was bound to get ahead." Sure, his son had just died in a swimming pool, but at least it was a very fancy pool.

The ambition and toil Calvinism requires will lead the economist Max Weber to coin the term "Protestant work ethic" to describe the Puritans' legacy of rolled-up sleeves. Tireless labor and ambition in pursuit of salvation, he opined, led to a culture of tireless labor and ambition and a new religion—capitalism. No wonder a German historian dubbed John Calvin "the virtual founder of America."

It makes sense that Winthrop, a man accustomed to setting lofty goals for himself, would then set lofty goals for the colony he is about to lead. "A Model of Christian Charity" is the blueprint of his communal aspirations. Standing before his shipmates, Winthrop stares down the Sermon on the Mount, as every Christian must.

Here, for example, is Martin Luther King, Jr., doing just that on November 17, 1957, in Montgomery's Dexter Avenue Baptist Church. He concluded the learned discourse that came to be known as the "loving your enemies" sermon this way: "So this morning, as I look into your eyes and into the eyes of all my brothers in Alabama and all over America and over the world, I say to you, 'I love you. I would rather die than hate you.'"

Go ahead and reread that. That is hands down the most beautiful, strange, impossible, but most of all radical thing a human being can say. And it comes from reading the most beautiful, strange, impossible, but most of all radical civics lesson ever taught, when Jesus of Nazareth went to a hill in Galilee and told his disciples, "Love your enemies, bless them that curse you, do good to them that hate you."

The Bible is a big long book and lord knows within its many mansions of eccentricity finding justification for literal and figurative witch hunts is as simple as pretending "enhanced investigation techniques" is not a synonym for torture. I happen to be with King in proclaiming the Sermon on the Mount's call for love to be at the heart of Christian behavior, and one of us got a Ph.D. in systematic theology.

"Man," Winthrop reminds his shipmates in "Christian

Charity," is "commanded to love his neighbor as himself." In the Semon on the Mount, Jesus puts the new in New Testament, informing his followers that they must do something way more difficult than being fond of the girl next door. Winthrop quotes him yet again. Matthew 5:44: "Love your enemies . . . do good to them that hate you." He also cites Romans 12:20: "If thine enemy hunger, feed him."

The colonists of Massachusetts Bay are not going to be any better at living up to this than any other government in Christendom. (Just ask the Pequot, or at least the ones the New Englanders didn't burn to death.) In fact, nobody can live up to this, but it's the mark of a Christlike Christian to know that he's supposed to.

Winthrop's future neighbors? Not so much. In fact, one of his ongoing difficulties as governor of the colony is going to be that his charges find him far too lenient. For instance, when one of his fellow Massachusetts Bay magistrates accuses Winthrop of dillydallying on punishment by letting some men who had been banished continue to hang around Boston, Winthrop points out that the men had been banished, not sentenced to be executed. And since they had been banished in the dead of winter, Winthrop let them stay until a thaw so that their eviction from Massachusetts wouldn't cause them to freeze to death on their way out of town. I can hear the threatening voice-over in his opponent's attack ad come the next election. *John Winthrop: soft on crime.*

This leads us to something undeniably remarkable: "A

Model of Christian Charity" was not written by a writer or a minister but rather by a governor. It isn't just a sermon, it is an act of leadership. And even if no one heard it, or no one was listening, it is, at the very least, a glimpse at what the chief executive officer of the Massachusetts Bay Colony believed he and this grumpy few before him were supposed to shoot for come dry land. Two words, he says: "justice and mercy."

For "a community of perils," writes Winthrop, "calls for extraordinary liberality." One cannot help but feel for this man. Here he is, pleading with Puritans to be flexible. In promoting what he calls "enlargement toward others," Winthrop has clearly thought through the possible pitfalls awaiting them on shore. He is worried about basic survival. He should be. He knows that half the Plymouth colonists perished in the first year. Thus he is reminding them of Christ's excruciating mandate to share. *If thine enemy hunger, feed him.*

Winthrop tells them that even if they have next to nothing, their faith commands them to give away everything. "If your brother be in want and you can help him . . . if you love God, you must help him."

When John Cotton's grandson, Cotton Mather, wrote his *Ecclesiastical History of New England* in 1702, he told a story about Winthrop that I would like to believe is true. In the middle of winter, Boston was low on fuel and a man came to the governor complaining that a "needy person" was stealing from his woodpile. Winthrop mustered the appropriate outrage and requested that the thief come see him, presumably for punishment. According to Mather, Winthrop tells the man,

> "Friend, it is a severe winter, and I doubt you are but meanly provided for wood; wherefore I would have you supply yourself at my woodpile till this cold season be over." And [Winthrop] then merrily asked his friends whether he had not effectually cured this man of stealing his wood.

If Mather's story is to be trusted, perhaps Winthrop was winking at Giles Tilleman. Tilleman is the "Cutler of Brussels" Winthrop mentions in "Christian Charity," along with other "forefathers in times of persecution" he would have heard of while reading John Foxe's *Book of Martyrs,* a popular compendium of the lives of Protestants who had been burned to death by Catholics for their beliefs. According to Foxe, when Tilleman saw the large pile of kindling that was to be used to burn him alive, he asked his executioner if most of the wood "might be given to the poor, saying, 'A small quantity will suffice to consume me.'"

In "Christian Charity," Winthrop asserts, "There is a time also when Christians . . . must give beyond their ability."

Winthrop asserts, "There is a time when a Christian must sell all and give to the poor, as they did in the Apostles' times." (It is so curious that this sermon, in my lifetime, would become so identified with the Communist-hating, Communist-baiting Ronald Reagan, considering Winthrop just proclaimed that a follower of Christ must be willing to renounce property. Utter Commie talk.)

After the Old Testament Israelites, the colonists' second-favorite biblical role models are the first-century churches founded by Christ's apostles and the missionary Paul. The small, local nature of churches such as those at Corinth and Ephesus is where the Puritans get their Congregationalist critique of Catholicism and the Church of England's Catholic power structure, in which local parishes are beholden to the dictates and whims of faraway bishops. In a Congregationalist church, the church members are answerable only to one another.

Winthrop quotes Corinthians. Which is to say, he quotes Paul's letter to the Corinth church admonishing the congregation to stop its bickering and heed Christ's words of love. Winthrop surely knows that the men and women before him heading to the boondocks of English territory are at least as capable of squabbling as any congregation in the provinces of Rome.

"Christ and his church make one body," Winthrop says, paraphrasing Paul (1 Corinthians 12:13 14: "For by one Spirit are we all baptized into one body. . . . For the body is not one member, but many"). Furthermore, claims Winthrop, "The ligaments of this body which knit together are love." Then he quotes Paul's letter to another church, in Galatia, "Bear ye one another's burdens and so fulfill the law of Christ."

This body of Christ, connected with the ligaments of

love, is not merely pretty poetry or spiritual mumbo jumbo to Winthrop and his people. It is a "bond of marriage between Him and us." Which is to say it is a contract. Remember, Winthrop was a lawyer. That might be why the final paragraphs of "Christian Charity," the ones that will be the most quoted later on, are the most profound. Given the task of outlining a binding legal pact between Massachusetts and God, Winthrop comes alive. "We are," he writes, "entered into covenant with Him for this work."

There is no concept a lawyer, especially an English one, cherishes more than that of precedent. And to Winthrop and his shipmates, the tradition of a covenant—a handshake deal between man and God in which man promises obedience and God grants salvation in return—extends, writes Perry Miller, "unbroken from Abraham to Boston."

"And I will make of thee a great nation," God had promised Abraham. The price of such greatness, as Cotton's farewell sermon already reminded the colonists, is a great big headache. Their duties, writes Winthrop, are these: "Now the only way to provide for our posterity, is to follow the counsel of Micah, to do justly, to love mercy, to walk humbly with our God." (Micah, an Old Testament prophet, said that God's words "do good to him that walketh uprightly"; as for God's promise to the sinners, "The mountains shall be molten under him, and the valleys shall be cleft, as wax before a fire.") Failures of justice, mercy, and humility, Winthrop warns, will cause God to "surely break out in wrath against us."

Winthrop uses a word to describe such a calamity that must have been especially terrifying if he was delivering this sermon at sea: shipwreck.

"The only way to avoid this shipwreck," he says, is to be "knit together in this work as one man."

Winthrop then utters one of the most beautiful sentences in the English language:

> We must delight in each other, make other's conditions
> our own, rejoice together, mourn together, labor and suf-
> fer together, always having before our eyes our commis-
> sion and community in the work, our community as
> members of the same body.

I am a reasonably happy-go-lucky person with a serviceable sense of humor and a nice-enough apartment in New York, the most exciting city in the world. Once I decided to devote years of my life to deciphering the thoughts and feelings of the dreary religious fanatics who founded New England nearly four hundred years ago, I was often asked at parties by my fellow New Yorkers the obvious question, "What are you working on?" When I would tell them a book about Puritans, they would often take a swig of the beer or bourbon in their hands and reply with either a sarcastic "Fun!" or a disdainful "Why?"

At which point, depending on my mood, I would either mumble something about my fondness for sermons as literature or mention taking my nephew to the *Mayflower* replica waterslide in a hotel pool in Plymouth. I would never answer with the honest truth. Namely, that in the weeks after two planes crashed into two skyscrapers here on the worst day of our lives, I found comfort in the words of Winthrop. When we were mourning together, when we were suffering together, I often thought of what he said and finally understood what he meant.

Perhaps my favorite of the countless times I broke into tears in the days following the attack, I watched citizens happily, patiently standing in a very long line. I marveled, remembering the time years earlier when a former president's motorcade had blocked Forty-second Street at rush hour and, forced to wait for ten whole minutes to cross to the other side, a businesswoman pointed at her watch and asked me, "Just who does he think he is?" and I answered, "I'm pretty sure he thinks he is the leader of the free world." But that long line of patient New Yorkers in 2001? They were giving blood.

We were breathing sooty air. The soot was composed of incinerated glass and steel but also, we knew, incinerated human flesh. When the local TV news announced that rescue workers sorting through the rubble in search of survivors were in need of toothpaste, half my block, having heard that there was finally something we could actually do besides worry and grieve, had already cleaned out the most popular name brands at the corner deli by the time I got there, so at the rescue workers' headquarters I sheepishly dropped off fourteen tubes of Sensodyne, the toothpaste for sensitive teeth.

We were members of the same body, breathing the cremated lungs of the dead and hoping to clean the teeth of the living.

The fact that Winthrop's words, so remarkable to me, were so apparently unremarkable to him and his people that his sermon did not bear mentioning, that neither he nor they recorded it in their diaries or letters home, makes me fond of him and them. Despite their unruly theology, their sometimes hair-trigger hate, the fact that the image of being members of the same body was so agreed upon to the point of cliché, makes them worth getting to know.

These English had affection for the Old Saxon word *weal*. It means wealth and riches but it means welfare and well-being, too. In "Christian Charity," Winthrop tells the colonists they must "partake of each other's strength and infirmity; joy and sorrow, weal and woe." Later on, Roger Williams would write, "There goes many a ship to sea, with many hundred souls in one ship, whose weal and woe is common, and is a true picture of a commonwealth, or a human combination or society."

This ideal will become so fundamental to the New England psyche that when the time comes for statehood, the citizens of Massachusetts do not become a state, but rather a commonwealth. John Adams put the following in the Commonwealth's Constitution:

The body politic is formed by a voluntary association of individuals: it is a social compact, by which the whole people covenants with each citizen, and each citizen with the whole people, that all shall be governed by certain laws for the common good.

Let's pause here amidst all the magic words like "commonwealth" and "common good" and savor what I like to call a snowball moment. There is a scene in the film *Reds* in which the two main characters, Jack Reed and Louise Bryant, American socialists in Moscow during the Russian Revolution, are caught up in the swirling, stirring romance of revolt. A whole people comes together to stand up for equality and brotherhood. Which sounds so very upstanding. But the genius of the film is that it also captures the giddy fun of that beginning. In a thrilling montage scored with a choral arrangement of the socialist anthem, "The Internationale," there is this one little flash, amongst the clips of Lenin at the podium or a workers' candlelight parade, in which Jack walks outside and Louise, lying in wait, pelts him with a snowball. It is a small snapshot that makes being part of a world historical uprising look like nothing but glee. Because what's coming has yet to come—the gulags and purges, Stalin and Mao, somewhere between 20 and 100 million dead. But at the snowball's moment of impact on Jack Reed's head, there is only happiness and hope.

That is where we are with Winthrop, at the grace note be-

fore the downbeat of gloom. Remember, when he delivers
"A Model of Christian Charity" he is either by the shore back
home or out on the open sea. He's been chosen governor
but he has yet to govern. What's coming has yet to come.
And here is what is coming:

On June 14, 1631, almost a year to the day after the *Arbella* arrives in Massachusetts, Governor Winthrop presides
over the court in Boston. He records in his journal that a servant named Philip Ratcliffe convicted of "most foul, scandalous invectives against our churches and government was
censured to be whipped, lose his ears, and be banished the
plantation, which was presently executed."

The Winthrop of "Christian Charity," yearning that the
settlers should think of themselves as members of the same
body, orders a man's ears to be cut off.

It reminds me of that moment in Whittaker Chambers's
book *Witness*. Chambers describes the way every decent
young person in the twentieth century contemplated becoming a Communist because of its ideal of fairness. But he
also describes the moment every decent person who became
a Communist stopped being one. A woman tells him that
her East German father had been a Communist Party loyal-
ist up until "One night—in Moscow—he heard screams." Yet
another person was being hauled off to jail in the dead of
night. Chambers writes, "Five annihilating words: one night
he heard screams."

As literature, Winthrop's "Christian Charity" is a kind of

poem of union—arm-in-arm romance, a snowball before the screams. But given Philip Ratcliffe's hacked-off ears, seemingly innocuous sentiments in the sermon come off as absolutely chilling. Like, "We must not look only on our own things, but also on the things of our brethren." One way to read that line is in keeping with the sermon's title, as a call for charity, a reminder to donate a few soup cans to the town food drive. But another way to read that line is to see it as a call not only for conformity but also surveillance—to keep watch on one's neighbors (or servants), to make sure they are not doing or saying anything that contradicts the government or the church. Same thing with Roger Williams's charming little metaphor about the commonwealth as a ship; it also has a sinister subtext, namely, that a ship has a captain and a captain's orders are to be obeyed.

Even such statements of Winthrop's as God "loves His elect because they are like Himself," and the early Christians "used to love any of their own religion even before they were acquainted with them," can be read as both a harmless ode to the affection shared by like-minded joiners *and* as a dangerous manifesto of xenophobia that cuts off the ears of anyone giving lip to those in charge. In that light, the opening sentence of the sermon seems even more ominous—that God made sure "some must be rich, some poor, some high and eminent in power and dignity; others mean and in subjection."

Here is a useful mantra for maintaining some basic em-

pathy for Winthrop and his English compatriots at their rac-
ist, persnickety, Indian-killing, puritanical worst: Harbottle
Grimstone. Their contemporary, Grimstone, or Grimston as
his name is sometimes spelled, was a Member of Parliament
from Colchester, and a relatively reasonable one at that.
Still, Harbottle Grimstone. Is there a creakier, more British
name? A name up there with ye olde Ralph of Coggeshall
or Hereward the Wake? A name that better sums up the
world and worldview the Puritans left behind? When I was
reading about Massachusetts Bay sending soldiers to burn
Pequot women and children alive I would mutter the
name "Harbottle Grimstone" under my breath to keep in
mind that these are more or less medieval people who are
chronologically closer to Chaucer's *Canterbury Tales* than to
The Wire.

It's worth revisiting New England's Puritans because
they are our medieval people. The most storied way to get
from the castle moat of monarchy to the polluted shoreline
of this here republic is on their dank little ships. We could
have done a lot worse. Perry Miller, thinking of Nathaniel
Hawthorne, wrote that having respect for the Puritans "is
not the same thing as believing in them."

As Hawthorne, who added an extra "w" to his last name
to distance himself from a forebear who had been a judge in
the Salem witch trials, put it, "Let us thank God for having
given us such ancestors; and let each successive generation

thank Him, not less fervently, for being one step further from them in the march of ages."

In "Christian Charity," Winthrop writes that if the colonists hold up their end of the covenant, their deity "will delight to dwell among us as His own people." They are not, therefore, merely living for God, they will live with Him.

"For we must consider that we shall be as a city upon a hill." Here, Winthrop has returned to the Sermon on the Mount. In Matthew 5:14, Jesus said to the throng before him, "Ye are the light of the world. A city that is set on a hill cannot be hid." This comes directly after Christ has enumerated the nine blessings called the beatitudes, including, "Blessed are the meek: for they shall inherit the earth." And "Blessed are the merciful: for they shall obtain mercy." And "Blessed are the peacemakers: for they shall be called the children of God."

"The eyes of all people are upon us," warned Winthrop, "so that if we shall deal falsely with our God in this work we have undertaken . . . we shall be made a story and a byword through the world."

The image of a city on a hill will get passed down as an all-American beacon of hope. But it wasn't only that to Winthrop. To him, the city on the hill was also something else, something worse—a warning. If he and his shipmates reneged on their covenant with God, the city on a hill would be a lighthouse of doom beckoning the wrath of God to Boston Harbor.

Talking about Winthrop's "A Model of Christian Charity" without discussing Ronald Reagan would be like mentioning Dolly Parton's "I Will Always Love You" and pretending Whitney Houston doesn't exist. Whitney and Reagan's covers were way more famous than the original versions ever were.

Winthrop's sermon, as a supposed early model for the idea of America, became a blank screen onto which Americans in general and Reagan in particular projected their own ideas about the country we ended up with. For a ten-year stretch, the 1980s, Winthrop's city on a hill became the national metaphor. And looking into the ways the sermon, or at least that one phrase in it, was used, throws open the American divide between action and words, between what we say we believe versus what we actually do.

Like a hostess dusting off her gravy boat come Thanksgiving, Ronald Reagan would trot out Winthrop's image of a city on a hill on special occasions throughout his political career. The night before winning the 1980 presidential election he proclaimed, "Let us resolve they will say of our day and our generation, we did keep the faith with our God, that we did act worthy of ourselves, that we did protect and pass on lovingly that shining city on a hill."

Reagan always brightened Winthrop's sound bite with the adjective "shining." The man was host of TV's *General*

Electric Theater for eight years, so it stands to reason he knew from luminosity. (He never shook off his old show-business sparkle, once referring to military uniforms as "wardrobe.")

In his reelection acceptance speech at the 1984 Republican National Convention, Reagan talked up his accomplishments of the preceding four years this way: "We raised a banner of bold colors—no pale pastels." (He is clearly ignoring all the pink slips flapping in the wind in his first term, what with 11.5 million Americans unemployed.)

He pressed on, "We proclaimed a dream of an America that would be a shining city on a hill." (As for real-life American cities, he told *Good Morning America* that year that homeless people who slept on grates were "homeless, you might say, by choice." He couldn't be more right—I have this fantasy that someday I'll throw off the shackles of my clean sheets and pillow-top mattress and curl up on a subway vent in the rain.)

Once, radio interviewer Terry Gross asked Bruce Springsteen about his hit song "Born in the U.S.A." and the '84 campaign, when President Reagan, during a stop in the singer's home state, said that America's future "rests in the message of hope in songs of a man so many young Americans admire, New Jersey's Bruce Springsteen."

Since "Born in the U.S.A." is about a Vietnam veteran who's been home from the war for ten years, remembering his dead comrades and complaining about not being able to get a job, Gross asked Springsteen if he thought his songs have "a message of hope."

"My songs are filled with hope," he answered. And in "Born in the U.S.A.," he explained, "The pride was in the chorus. . . . In my songs . . . the hope part is in the choruses. The blues . . . your daily realities . . . are in the verses." Even the famously forgetful Reagan could remember the chorus; it consists of the line "Born in the U.S.A." repeated four times. The verses have lines that speak to what actually *living* in the U.S.A. can be like, such as "You end up like a dog that's been beat too much," or "Down in the shadow of the penitentiary."

Born in the U.S.A. was the number one album on the Billboard chart on July 16, 1984, when Mario Cuomo gave the keynote speech at the Democratic National Convention in San Francisco titled "A Tale of Two Cities." Cuomo, then governor of New York, scrutinized President Reagan's favorite metaphor.

"A shining city is perhaps all the president sees from the portico of the White House and the veranda of his ranch, where everyone seems to be doing well," Cuomo supposed. "But there's another city; there's another part to the shining city." He spoke directly to Reagan:

Maybe, maybe, Mr. President, if you visited some more places; maybe if you went to Appalachia, where some people still live in sheds; maybe if you went to Lackawanna, where thousands of unemployed steelworkers wonder why we subsidized foreign steel. Maybe—Maybe, Mr. President, if you stopped in at a shelter in Chicago and spoke to the homeless there; maybe, Mr. President, if you asked a woman who had been denied the help she needed to feed her children because you said you needed the money for a tax break for a millionaire or for a missile we couldn't afford to use.

Cuomo, obviously, sings the blues. He points out that the country is in "the worst recession since 1932," and that the two-hundred-billion-dollar federal budget deficit is the "largest in the history of the universe." He blurts, "We give money to Latin American governments that murder nuns, and then we lie about it." He channels Winthrop and defines a proper government as "the sharing of benefits and burdens for the good of all, feeling one another's pain, sharing one another's blessings."

Then, addressing his fellow Democrats before him, he proclaims:

We must get the American public to look past the glitter, beyond the showmanship to the reality, the hard substance of things. And we'll do it not so much with speeches that sound good as with speeches that are good and sound; not so much with speeches that will bring people to their feet as with speeches that will bring people to their senses. We

must make—We must make the American people hear our
"Tale of Two Cities." We must convince them that we don't
have to settle for two cities, that we can have one city, indi-
visible, shining for all of its people.

The party's mild-mannered presidential nominee, Walter
Mondale, echoed Cuomo later in the campaign, again trying to
wrestle Winthrop from Reagan, calling for the country to end
the "selfishness" and "greed" of the previous four years. "Winthrop said," remarked Mondale, that "to be a shining city on the
hill, we must strengthen, defend, preserve and comfort one
another. We must rejoice together, mourn together, labor and
suffer together. We must be knit together by a bond of love."

So, which Winthrop did Americans elect—the suffering
blues singer in mourning or the pop star from the shining
city? The only state Mondale won was Minnesota, where he
was from. Reagan swept *the other forty-nine.*

In the U.S.A., we want to sing along with the chorus and
ignore the verses, ignore the blues. That is why the "city on
a hill" is the image from Winthrop's speech that stuck and
not "members of the same body." No one is going to hold up
a cigarette lighter in a stadium to the tune of "mourn together, suffer together." City on a hill, though—that has a
backbeat we can dance to. And that's why the citizens of the
United States not only elected and reelected Ronald Reagan;
that's why we *are* Ronald Reagan.

Remember this? In 1987, when President Reagan finally

went on national TV to apologize for his underlings' secret and illegal weapons sales to Iran in exchange for hostages and to purchase weapons for anticommunist Nicaraguan death squads, he said, "A few months ago I told the American people I did not trade arms for hostages. My heart and my best intentions still tell me that's true, but the facts and evidence tell me it is not."

By the time Reagan delivered his farewell address on January 11, 1989, I was a college radio newscaster at KGLT in Bozeman, Montana, cutting reel-to-reel tape from the AP feed. I'll never again have a job that cathartic, literally slicing the news with a razor blade. Once sliced and spliced, Reagan's self-congratulatory benediction went out to the station's listeners, including students, ranchers, minimum-wage dishwashers, skiers driving up to Bridger Bowl, guys in bands who were trying to decide whether or not to move to Seattle, and members of the community food co-op who would rant with equal fervor against organized religion and refined sugar.

In his speech, Reagan brought up John Winthrop yet again, calling the Puritan governor "an early freedom man" from whom he got his sound bite about the city on a hill. He continued:

> I've spoken of the shining city all my political life, but I
> don't know if I ever quite communicated what I saw when
> I said it. But in my mind, it was a tall proud city built on
> rocks stronger than oceans, wind-swept, God-blessed,

and teeming with people of all kinds living in harmony and peace, a city with free ports that hummed with commerce and creativity, and if there had to be city walls, the walls had doors and the doors were open to anyone with the will and the heart to get here. That's how I saw it, and see it still.

And how stands the city on this winter night? More prosperous, more secure, and happier than it was eight years ago. But more than that, after two hundred years, two centuries, she still stands strong and true on the granite ridge, and her glow has held steady no matter what storm.

My heart told me that wasn't true. The facts and evidence also told me that wasn't true.

Remember Winthrop's city? Where "the rich and mighty should not eat up the poor"? Where "if thy brother be in want and thou canst help him . . . if thou lovest God thou must help him"?

President Reagan did not utter the word "AIDS" in public until more than 20,000 people had died from the disease. His appointed officials embezzled funds earmarked for cleaning up toxic waste sites and gave the money to Republican candidates. He cut school lunch programs for needy children. He fired 11,345 striking air traffic controllers, which, according to the *Village Voice,* led to 253 deaths due to controller errors over the next ten years. He cut the budget for the Department of Housing and Urban Development from $32 billion in 1981 to $7.5 billion in 1988; two million Americans were homeless by 1989. The only federal department whose budget was not cut, but increased, was the Department of Defense; that was because the president's white whale was the Soviet Union. Being ready and able to bomb the hell out of the evil empire was the nation's top priority and if that meant thousands of poor kids had to skip lunch or sleep in cars in poisoned neighborhoods, so be it.

The statistics above are alarming enough. But the way Reagan not only ignored the facts—the truth didn't *feel* true—but simply said that all was shiny in the city of his mind, was extra galling. As Abraham Lincoln put it in an exasperated letter to his friend Joshua Speed in 1855, complaining about slavery and religious intolerance, he would "prefer emigrating to some country where they make no pretense of loving liberty—to Russia, for instance, where despotism can be taken pure and without the base alloy of hypocrisy."

A few weeks after Reagan's 1989 farewell address aired, a new Elvis Costello album showed up at the radio station and the DJs wore out the grooves on "Tramp the Dirt Down," in which the singer hoped he would live long enough to see the death of Reagan's transatlantic best friend, Margaret Thatcher, so he could jump up and down on her grave. I confess that became my Reagan fantasy, too. Until his ghastly, slow death from Alzheimer's disease deprived any detractor with half a heart of even that petty, dirt-tramping thrill.

In 2004, I did watch Reagan's funeral at the National Cathedral on live TV. The ailing Thatcher sent a video eulogy, quoting Arnold Bennett that Reagan personified "the great cause of cheering us all up."

Former senator John C. Danforth gave the homily, reading from that part of the Gospel of Matthew from which Winthrop himself cribbed the city-on-a-hill image: "You are the light of the world. A city on a hill cannot be hid." Danforth continued:

> Winthrop believed that the eyes of the world would be on America because God had given us a special commission, so it was our duty to shine forth. The Winthrop message became the Reagan message. It rang of optimism, and we longed to hear it, especially after the dark years of Vietnam and Watergate. It was a vision with policy implications.
>
> America could not hide its light under a bushel. It could not turn in on itself and hunker down. Isolationism was not an option. Neither was protectionism. We must champion freedom everywhere. We must be the beacon for the world.

Danforth went on to say, "If ever we have known a child of light, it was Ronald Reagan. He was aglow with it. He had no dark side, no scary hidden agenda."

Maybe some of the people there pictured the late president's winning smile and smiled themselves. I just sat there frowning on my couch, picturing secret crates of weapons being unloaded from a cargo plane in Iran to pay for secret crates of weapons being unloaded from a cargo plane in Nicaragua.

Sandra Day O'Connor read an excerpt from Winthrop's "A Model of Christian Charity." She reminded the congregation, "The city on the hill passage was referenced by President Reagan in several notable speeches." Appointed by Reagan, O'Connor was the first woman to serve on the Supreme Court, and thus an obvious choice to speak at his memorial service.

John Winthrop, however, must have been rolling over in his grave, wondering when did women become magistrates and how come one of them is reading his sermon, considering he was the man who barked at female heretic Anne Hutchinson, "We are your judges and not you ours."

O'Connor read slowly, her voice small and grave. She sounded like an old woman whose friend has died. She will pause slightly when she gets to the word "mourn." The text was edited beforehand. This is everything she read:

> Now, the only way to provide for posterity is to follow the counsel of Micah: to do justly, to love mercy, to walk humbly with our God.
>
> We must delight in each other, make others' conditions our own, rejoice together, mourn together, labor and suffer together, always having before our eyes our

commission and community in the work as members of the same body.

The Lord will be our God and delight to dwell among us as his own people.

For we must consider that we shall be as a city upon a hill. The eyes of all people are upon us so that if we shall deal falsely with our God in this work we have undertaken and so cause him to withdraw his present help from us, we shall be made a story and a byword through the world.

At that moment, there was one story known through the world, a byword on everyone's lips: Abu Ghraib. A couple of weeks before O'Connor said that last line, I went to New York University to hear a speech given by one of the people sitting there in the National Cathedral—former vice president Al Gore—demanding that another person sitting there—Defense Secretary Donald Rumsfeld—resign because of the revelation that American Military Police officers had tortured, raped, and killed Iraqi prisoners at Baghdad's Abu Ghraib penitentiary.

Everyone in the cathedral, everyone watching on television, hearing O'Connor's voice, had seen the appalling photos—naked prisoners made to pile themselves into a human pyramid as their American captors stood behind them, smiling at the camera and making the "thumbs-up" sign; prisoners made to line up for snapshots of their genitalia; prisoners bleeding because they had been bitten by dogs.

In his NYU speech, Gore asked of Rumsfeld and the president he serves (who would of course also be there amongst them at Reagan's funeral), "How dare they drag the good name of the United States of America through the mud of Saddam Hussein's torture prison?"

Like Winthrop, like Reagan, like Danforth at Reagan's funeral, Gore cited the Sermon on the Mount. "In my religious tradition," he remarked, "I have been taught that . . . 'a corrupt tree bringeth forth evil fruit. . . . Wherefore by their fruits ye shall know them.'"

Gore even implied that these crimes against Iraqi prisoners of war were an offense not just to us, right now, but to our Puritan forebears:

> What a terrible irony that our country, which was founded by refugees seeking religious freedom—coming to America to escape domineering leaders who tried to get them to renounce their religion—would now be responsible for this kind of abuse.
>
> Ameen Saeed al-Sheikh told the *Washington Post* that he was tortured and ordered to denounce Islam. And after his leg was broken one of his torturers started hitting it while ordering him to curse Islam and then, "They ordered me to thank Jesus that I'm alive."

Gore used the argument of American exceptionalism (first set forth by John Cotton and John Winthrop and their comrades) to bemoan this betrayal of American exceptionalism—how we as a people "consistently choose good over evil in our collective aspirations more than the people of any other nation," how Lincoln, early on in the Civil War, called for saving the Union because it was the "last best hope of earth."

That was the speech in which Lincoln pointed out "we cannot escape history." Well, we can't. I can't really fault Gore for saying that what happened at Abu Ghraib is sickening, not only because it's just plain sickening but because America is supposed to be better than that. No: best. I hate to admit it, but I still believe that, too. Because even though my head tells me that the idea that America was chosen by God as His righteous city on a hill is ridiculous, my heart still buys into it. And I don't even believe in God! And I have heard the screams! Why is America the last best hope of Earth? What if it's Liechtenstein? Or, worse, Canada?

The thing that appeals to me about Winthrop's "Christian Charity" and Cotton's "God's Promise to His Plantation" from this end of history is that at least the arrogant ballyhoo that New England is special and chosen by God is tempered by the self-loathing Puritans' sense of reckoning. The same wakefulness the individual Calvinist was to use to keep watch over his own sins Winthrop and Cotton called for also in the group at large. This humility, this fear, was what kept their delusions of grandeur in check. That's what subsequent generations lost. From New England's Puritans we inherited the idea that America is blessed and ordained by God above all nations, but lost the fear of wrath and retribution.

The eyes of all people are upon us. And all they see is a mash-up of naked prisoners and an American girl in fatigues standing there giving a thumbs-up. As I write this, the United States of America is still a city on a hill; and it's still shining—because we never turn off the lights in our torture prisons. That's how we carry out the sleep deprivation.

At the Massachusetts State Archives in Boston, Assistant Archivist Michael Comeau shows me the most important item John Winthrop packed in his luggage on the *Arbella*—the Charter of the Massachusetts Bay Company granted by King Charles I. Comeau points to the "bug-eyed" portrait of Charles lording over the upper-left-hand corner of the first page.

There is a little hole above Charles's head, but otherwise the document is in terrific shape. I ask Comeau if that has anything to do with the New Englanders' sense of historic self-importance. "Oh my god," he answers, "these people killed themselves to make sure there was a paper trail." In fact, not only did they take excellent care of the Charter itself, they saved the original beeswax seal. He opens a box containing some brown globs he admits "look like a cow pie. At the time it would have been a vibrant red. Now it looks like dirt."

The beginning of the Charter alludes to the evolution of

the Massachusetts Bay Company, how King James, Charles's father, gave patents for land in New England dating back to 1607 to the Virginia Company of Plymouth, which turned into the Council of New England, which turned into the Massachusetts Bay Company. I'm guessing part of the point of this is to reassure Charles that he is not condoning some newfangled religious experiment but rather continuing to support a practical, moneymaking venture approved by his father. The Charter butters up Charles by referring to his dad as "our most dear and royal father, King James, of blessed memory."

The Charter authorized the Massachusetts Bay Company to colonize all the land between three miles north of the Merrimack River and three miles south of the Charles River, stretching "from sea to sea" (i.e., all the way to the Pacific), including "soils, grounds, havens, ports, rivers, waters, fishing, mines, any minerals, as well royal mines of gold and silver, as other mines and minerals, precious stones, quarries, and all and singular other commodities" therein. Just so long as the company's executives make no laws "contrary or re pugnant to the laws and statutes" of England.

At this point in the story of the founding of Massachusetts Bay, many accounts have a lot of folksy fun with a yarn about how sneaky it was of the Massachusetts Bay Company to "forget" to put into the Charter that the document remain in England, and that the company's administrative meetings must also be held in England as previous charters had. This allows the company to take the Charter with them abroad, making self-government in Massachusetts possible with little royal oversight. In that scenario, says Michael the archivist, "Winthrop steals the Charter in the dark of night." So the founding of Massachusetts becomes a Bugs Bunny cartoon— King Charles, in hunting cap, is outsmarted by the wascally Winthrop.

Our folksy fun, however, is ruined by annoying scholars whose painstaking hard work has uncovered the murkier, less dramatic truth, requiring footnotes about the Third Charter of Virginia of 1612 or the East India Company's royal charter of 1600 allowing its officers to meet "in such convenient place" they "shall think fit." Librarian Ronald Dale Karr writes, "The omission of a designated meeting place in the Massachusetts Bay Charter of 1629 was thus neither unprecedented nor unusual." This debunks, says Michael, the myth of "the deviousness of Winthrop."

If the potential for colonial self-government wasn't exactly new, Winthrop and Co. still exploited this loophole like none before them had dared.

One innovation in the Charter does afford Americans front-row seats at the birth of the national pastime— regularly scheduled voting. The Charter states that the Massachusetts governor, deputy governor, and the representatives known as "assistants" are to be voted in or out every spring. Historian Samuel Eliot Morison opined, "The particular feature of this charter which proved so successful and enduring as to become an American institution was the principle of stated elections." This is, he continues, "in contrast to the English or parliamentary system."

This is still true. As an American, I am entirely flummoxed by the willy-nilly process by which the Brits acquire a new prime minister. It seems like one afternoon after tea they decide to get rid of the old one, then the majority party in the House of Commons picks the person they most want to yell at on C-SPAN's *Prime Minister's Questions,* then the new prime minister goes to Buckingham Palace and for two minutes the whole country politely pretends he was the queen's idea.

U.S. citizens can thank the Massachusetts Bay colonists for breaking with that tradition. While Americans choose a new president in a process that is as insane as the way the United Kingdom ends up with a new prime minister—given the fact that the Electoral College makes sure our president is chosen by three counties in Florida and Ohio (or nine Supreme Court justices)—at least we can print "Election Day" in our calendars ahead of time. And looking forward to that date circled in November can get a citizen through a lot of cold nights. As Morison noted, the Massachusetts Bay's "corporate mode of election put an almost continuous check on both executive officers and representatives. It became an essential principle of every state constitution and the federal constitution."

The Massachusetts Bay Colony becomes, under this Charter, a sort of republic—the most severely limited, totalitarian, closed-minded, vindictive, hard-ass republic possible.

But the democratic impulse is a mutating virus that adapts and changes, quickens and grows; it is contagious, and the Charter is one important sneeze.

At first, the General Court in 1630 consisted of eight people—the governor, the deputy governor, and six other magistrates called assistants. But within a year, a hundred others, church members all, known as "freemen," are sworn in to court; they are granted the power to elect the assistants, who in turn elect the governor. But by 1632, the freemen raise a stink and are allowed to elect the governor directly. They are, however, required to take an oath that they will be "obedient" to the governor and assistants. They also pledge to rat out their neighbors by alerting the governor and assistants "of any sedition, violence, treachery, or other hurt or evil which I shall know, hear, or vehemently suspect to be plotted or intended against the said commonwealth, or the said government established."

The vow of obedience and that thing about vehement suspicions doesn't exactly make the democratic idealist in me want to hum the trombone part from "Stars and Stripes Forever." Still, got to start somewhere. So it's worth celebrating, a little, that within two years of the Massachusetts Bay Company's arrival on these shores, a hundred white male religious fanatics get to pick their own dictator in a show of hands. Winthrop will be that dictator on and off until he dies.

Winthrop and the other assistants get their authoritarianism from the same place they derive all their other beliefs—the Bible. Winthrop railed, "If we should change from a mixed aristocracy to mere democracy, first we should have no warrant in Scripture for it for there was no such government in Israel." He continues, calling democracy "the meanest and worst of all forms of government . . . a manifest breach of the Fifth Commandment."

The Fifth Commandment is honor your father and mother. To these people, "father and mother" are not merely biological parents. Martin Luther wrote the best explanation of how the Fifth Commandment extends beyond the nuclear family and into public life:

> In this commandment belongs a further statement regarding all kinds of obedience to persons in authority who have to command and govern. For all authority flows and is propagated from the authority of parents. . . . They are all called fathers in the Scriptures, as those who in their government perform the functions of a father, and should have a paternal heart toward their subordinates.

That explanation goes a long way toward explaining Winthrop's seemingly schizophrenic behavior. By setting limits on dissent, Winthrop's government is facing a question asked of and by every government. But according to the Puritans' interpretation of the Fifth Commandment, a governor is also a patriarch. This requires tough love, but love nonetheless. How the Fifth Commandment informs Winthrop's conduct is best explained in the person of Philip Ratcliffe, he of the sliced-off ears.

Recall that Winthrop was one of the magistrates who convicted Ratcliffe of "scandalous invectives against our churches and government." Which is to say Ratcliffe broke the Fifth Commandment twice over by failing to honor both his church fathers and his legislative/judicial fathers of the General Court. His punishment, besides the ear lopping and a whipping, is banishment.

Earlier, I mentioned in passing that throughout his tenure as governor, the townspeople accused Winthrop of leniency. The example I gave was the Bostonians' disgust that Winthrop allowed a couple of men who had been banished to loiter in Boston. Winthrop's reasoning was that "being in the winter, they must otherwise have perished" if they were forced to hike into the icy wilderness right away.

Well, Ratcliffe was one of those men Winthrop refused to kick out into the cold. And I think it's because Winthrop takes the Fifth Commandment seriously. He sees himself as a father and the other colonists as his children. Is this condescending? Absolutely. Does it explain his contradictory words and deeds, the disconnect between the ideal of the colonists being "members of the same body" and chopping off a loudmouth's ears? I think it does. A father sometimes plays the doting dad who buys his son a Popsicle, or he can be the furious punisher of the phrase "wait until your father gets home." By banishing Ratcliffe, Winthrop was disowning him; by letting Ratcliffe stay in Boston until the weather warmed up, Winthrop was looking out for his safety. Winthrop was one of those parents who never wants to see his kid again but drives him to the bus station to make sure he leaves town warm and dry.

A settler named Thomas Wiggin described Winthrop as "ruling with much mildness" toward the law-abiding. As for troublemakers, Wiggin claimed Winthrop was "strict in execution of Justice . . . to the terror of offenders."

If the Fifth Commandment accounts for Winthrop and his fellow magistrates' style of governing, I think it also explains their conciliatory attitudes toward the monarchy and the Church of England—why they are not Separatists like their neighbors in Plymouth. Remember the "Humble Request," the open letter the colonists sent to King Charles and the Church before their departure? It was addressed to "Reverend Fathers." It called the Church of England "our dear mother," proclaiming that their hope for salvation "we have received in her bosom and sucked it from her breasts."

Also recall the Charter's description of King James as "our most dear and royal father."

This paternal and maternal language is not mere empty words to these Puritans. They believe the Fifth Commandment requires them to obey the parental authority of king and church. Or at least appear to.

At the Massachusetts Historical Society in Boston, I visit the reading room. It's like a cartoon of East Coast finery: dark wood paneling, oil paintings on the wall of illustrious, staring Bostonians whose eyes accuse visitors who went to state schools west of the Mississippi, "You're not from around here, are you?"

I was there to read John Winthrop's journal. The actual thing. It's hard not to look at the water stains and imagine they came from Atlantic sea spray during the crossing. I don't think Winthrop was any more nervous leaving England than I was leafing through such a brittle, wrinkly, nearly four-hundred-year-old book.

The library assistant, who was helpful and diligent, bordering on liturgical, handed me the first volume, then the third, wincing that the second volume "burned up in a fire." Which happened nearly two hundred years ago, but this true-blue young archivist is still in mourning.

Winthrop's handwriting was so dreadful I could only make out a handful of words, from *"Arbella"* on the first page to a "godly" here and a "temptations" there. There is an autograph, "Your loving son, John Winthrop," pasted in at the end of the third volume by a Winthrop heir who found the signature from Winthrop Jr. to his father and didn't want it to get lost. For some reason that made them both seem so alive and so odd—to follow an endearment like "your loving son" with a last name, being simultaneously heartfelt and formal—much like Winthrop himself. (The younger Winthrop's hand is also represented in the first volume's endpapers, where he drew plans for houses and forts for his father.)

I found myself fixated on the third volume's sad, blank pages when the diary stops cold in 1649. That's when Winthrop died. I stared at all that yellowing emptiness and remembered seeing the globe in Will Rogers's office when I toured his house in Santa Monica; there are pencil marks all over it that Rogers, an avid aviator, made when he was planning his flights around the world, and it's just so poignant to see those lines, since he died in a plane crash, but it's even more poignant to think about a kid from Oklahoma who parlayed a few jokes and rope tricks into seeing the world. Just as it is touching to look at Winthrop's drawings in his diary of the coastlines of Maine and Massachusetts, sketched from the deck of the *Arbella,* and marvel at how far he had come and wonder if he was concentrating on the contours of the shoreline to take his mind off his fear of actually stepping onto the strange new continent before him and commencing his strange new life.

Luckily, the Massachusetts Historical Society has published the entirety of Winthrop's journals, including the unfortunate second volume, which had already been transcribed before the blaze.

The first journal's endpapers, where Winthrop jotted down odds and ends of information in preparing for the Atlantic crossing in 1630, document the extremes of what he had on his mind before leaving home.

Winthrop writes down instructions for making gunpowder, putting up a chimney, and building a small boat. He makes lists of the provisions for the voyage, including thirty bushels of oatmeal, forty bushels of peas, two wooden bowls, two barrels of cider, the equivalent of ten thousand gallons of beer, 138 wooden spoons, and "11 Ferkins of Butter," a ferkin (or firkin) being a "unit of capacity," according to my dictionary, "equal to half a kilderkin." (That clears that up.)

But Winthrop also jots down a list of Bible verses having to do with charity and generosity that he will refer to when he writes "A Model of Christian Charity." These passages include "Give to him that asketh thee" from the Sermon on the Mount; and Isaiah 58, which touts that for those who give their bread to the hungry and clothe the naked, "thine health shall spring forth speedily; and 2 Corinthians 9:7, in which "God loveth a cheerful giver."

In other words, after Winthrop has acquired all his butter firkins, food stirrers, and beer, along with six dozen candles, twenty thousand biscuits, and twenty-nine sides of beef, he goes through the Bible and writes down a bunch of verses commanding him to be willing to cheerfully give all that stuff away. *My firkin is your firkin* being one of Christianity's primary creeds. He is simultaneously imagining an idealistic city on a hill, and making sure that city has nine hundred pounds of cheese.

Winthrop's journal proper begins on March 29, 1630, "near the Isle of Wight, in the *Arbella,* a ship of three hundred and fifty tons." Named for one of Winthrop's shipmates, the highfalutin Lady Arbella Johnson, the *Arbella* and the other vessels in the fleet will not reach open sea for nearly two weeks, working their way past Yarmouth and Plymouth and the Isles of Scilly off England's southwest coast. Before then, Winthrop will witness a Dutch ship get stuck on a rock. He will have breakfast with the caretaker of Yarmouth Castle, an "old sea captain in Queen Elizabeth's time." He will bemoan that his son Henry, who had gone ashore for cows, was unable to rejoin the *Arbella* because of high winds—his only hope being that Henry can hitch a ride with one of the other New England–bound vessels. (He does.) And if that's not enough to worry about, with eight possibly Spanish ships approaching, Winthrop almost goes to war. The Lady Arbella and the other women and children are sent belowdecks. The men get out their weapons, which is to say they fetched their muskets and "went to prayer upon the upper deck." In the end, they were not enemy ships, "and so," writes Winthrop, "(God be praised) our fear and danger was turned into mirth and friendly entertainment."

His notes on the Atlantic crossing are so detailed in terms of position and wind direction- -N by NW, S by SW, etc.— that one could probably re-create the *Arbella*'s route fairly accurately. And by "one" I do not mean me. I get seasick on the ferry to Weehawken. I think I would have preferred be-

ing burned at the stake in England to sailing to America because the best thing about death by fire is that it tends to be
so nice and dry. I've always loved the story of the founding of
New England for the same reason I have a thing for surfing
movies and *Moby-Dick*—I'm afraid of water, so the only thing
I'll dive into is a narrative account.

To see a ship similar to the *Arbella,* you can go to Plymouth, Mass., and climb aboard the replica *Mayflower II,* which
to me is a claustrophobic floating vomitorium I couldn't
stand to be on for more than nine minutes, much less nine
weeks. (A replica *Arbella* was built for Massachusetts' 300th
anniversary in 1930; but, according to Francis Bremer, it
ended up beached at Salem's Pioneer Village and the city of
Salem tore the thing down after it "became a haunt for youths
indulging in various questionable activities." Winthrop would
surely approve of this crackdown, having mused in his journal
during the Atlantic crossing that a servant girl got drunk because it is "a common fault in our young people, that they
gave themselves to drink hot waters very immoderately.")

In terms of historical tourism, the Pilgrims of 1620 get
all the glory. Families, my own included, plan vacations
around visiting Plymouth's *Mayflower II* and "Plimoth Plantation," the re-created colonial English and Wampanoag
village on the outskirts of town. My sister Amy, my then-
seven-year-old nephew Owen, and I visited it one summer.
It is peopled by actors who will not, under any circum-
stances, break character—not even when Owen suggested

they could really spruce up their cramped little houses by shopping at Home Depot or maybe Lowe's because Lowe's offers "everyday low prices." We strolled around the dusty paths among men and women in colorful seventeenth-century garb. (When Owen asked a woman in a blue skirt why she wasn't wearing black like Pilgrims are supposed to, she said that only rich people wear black, and then sneered at me and my ripped black T-shirt as if I were Marie Antoinette.) We then made the acquaintance of one Englishman Amy dubbed the "Pilgrim Archie Bunker." We had just ambled through the Wampanoag village and watched a woman cooking with a clay pot, so Owen had indigenous people on his mind. He told Archie about his collection of Hopi and Navajo kachina dolls he started the previous summer when we went to the Grand Canyon. After an annoying back-and-forth in which Archie determined we apparently came from New Spain and were therefore suspected of Catholicism, we returned to the subject of kachinas. Archie backed away from Owen and asked him if they're poppets. No, Owen said, "Not puppets—wood carvings." I told him a poppet is a doll used in witchcraft. "You know, like when Scooby-Doo goes to Salem." Owen shook his head at Archie and said, "Kachinas are gods, Hopi and Navajo gods." Archie pointed his finger at Owen's chest and raised his voice, "Not the true God Jesus Christ!" Then he told Owen he's never shot an Indian personally but he wouldn't lose any sleep over it if he did, and that he would trade with the Indians, though he would never give them anything of value, perhaps "a pot that was full of holes." Then my sister grabbed Owen by the arm and said, "Come on, Owen. Let's get out of here before Mama punches a Pilgrim."

I used to feel a little sorry for the Massachusetts Bay colonists of 1630, whose story is told, if at all, in negligible plaques and statues no Bostonian notices on the way to work. Plymouth has Plymouth Rock, and Boston has, in a glass case at the State House, "one of the oldest upholstered chairs made in New England"—an item that doesn't lend itself to cries of "Honey, pack up the car." One reason for that is that the Boston founders were more successful city builders. Which stands to reason, since they weren't just building a city. They were building a city on a hill. Unlike Plymouth, which is beholden to the Pilgrims to this day for its livelihood because nothing much happened in that town after its original settlers died. Which is why the Plymouth Colony was actually absorbed into the Massachusetts Bay Colony in 1691. Boston, with its fine harbor, kept moving and growing and building right on top of the Winthrop fleet's foundations. Literally: the office building that was Boston's first steel-frame "skyscraper" was built in 1893 on top of the site of Winthrop's Boston house.

Plus, having been to Plymouth, I now feel confident that Winthrop and his shipmates would appreciate being spared the indignity of fame. I am thinking specifically of the *Mayflower* replica with a waterslide jutting from its deck in the Pilgrim Cove Pool at Plymouth's John Carver Inn.

Would William Bradford, who wrote of the *Mayflower's* voyage that "many were afflicted with seasickness," ever stop throwing up if he spent an afternoon watching my nephew come shooting out of the ship's slide, giggling, over and over again, each time making a loud, highly chlorinated splash? Would Bradford point out that half the *Mayflower* passengers died their first year in Plymouth so maybe it's disrespectful to turn the vessel into a cannonball-launcher next to a hot tub? Or that he and the other Pilgrims came over on the real *Mayflower* to follow rules more profound than "Do Not Slide Head First"?

During Winthrop's two months on the Atlantic, he writes of the cold and the fog. There are tempests. There are days when the sea is "beating us back as much as the wind put us forward." He sees a whale. The slovenly crew keeps the gun deck in "beastly" disorder, so Winthrop and the other officers organize a cleaning schedule. Some sick children are made to hold on to a rope in the sunshine to air them out. June 7 was a day of extreme emotional non sequiturs, in which Winthrop notes the passengers caught twenty-six cod, "so we all feasted with fish this day. A woman was delivered of a child in our ship, stillborn."

Then, the next day, land ho. They could see Mount Desert Island off the coast of Maine. "And there came a smell off the shore like the smell of a garden," Winthrop wrote.

For four days, they followed the coastline down. At four o'clock in the morning, on Saturday, June 12, they reached Cape Ann. Some Salem men, including John Endecott, came out in boats to fetch them. Endecott was the Massachusetts Bay Company's advance man. He had led a small group of pioneers to America two years earlier to prepare the way for large-scale settlement. So that evening, Endecott and his fellows fed Winthrop supper in Salem, "a good venison pasty and good beer."

Compare that reception to William Bradford's description of the *Mayflower*'s landfall at Cape Cod ten years earlier. The Pilgrims were overjoyed that they had finally made it for, oh, two minutes, until they realized that "they had no friends to welcome them nor inns to entertain or refresh their weatherbeaten bodies; no houses or much less towns to repair to, to seek for succor."

Then again, John Endecott is Winthrop's Welcome Wagon rep. Endecott does not go down in history for his warmth. Nathaniel Hawthorne describes him as "the Puritan of Puritans," a man "so stern" that he "seemed wrought of iron." Later on, Endecott will send Governor Winthrop a letter complaining about how it's frowned upon for a justice of the peace to hit someone. Because Endecott, a justice of the peace, has just punched a defendant—in court. "If you had seen the manner of his carriage," continues Endecott, "with such daring of me, with his arms akimbo, it would have provoked a very patient man." He says that if it were suddenly legal for a judge to go around clocking people, "you should not hear me complain."

So besides being cranky and pugilistic, Endecott has been the man in charge in Massachusetts Bay up until the moment Winthrop gets there with the Charter and usurps him. On Boston Common there is a relief sculpture called the Founders Memorial that pictures the two men shaking hands on the shore, with the *Arbella* in the harbor behind them. In it, some of the men and women who have just disembarked from the ship, as well as a pair of Indians off to the side, witness this significant occasion as if all is well and good. But Endecott can't have been entirely thrilled with his sudden demotion.

Back at the Massachusetts State Archives, Michael Comeau had shown me the copy of the Massachusetts Charter given to Endecott. It is marked "dupl," indicating it is a duplicate, place-holder charter. But still, said Comeau, "Legend has it Endecott would wield it like a scepter."

Endecott would remain the mullah of Salem, which might have something to do with that town's touchy religious climate throughout the seventeenth century. The passengers of the Winthrop fleet did not stick around. Deputy Governor Thomas Dudley later wrote, "Salem, where we landed, pleased us not."

So the colonists dispersed south, breaking off into various settlements such as Roxbury and Dorchester, Boston neighborhoods that would become famous in the twentieth century for race riots and the boy band New Kids on the Block.

Winthrop moved to Charlestown, just across the Charles River from what would become Boston, living in a structure that was part bachelor pad, part town hall, and that everyone called the Great House, probably because there wasn't a lot of competition in the architectural excellence department.

The New England Puritans are not remembered for their sweetness, and yet there was much sweetness in them. This is especially true of Winthrop. For instance, he sailed to Massachusetts alone to get settled. Until he could send for his wife, Margaret, he wrote her a letter proposing that they think of each other at a specific time twice a week, a sort of steady date on the astral plane. He promised, "Mondays and Fridays, at five of the clock at night, we shall meet in spirit till we meet in person." But Winthrop is so busy his first few months in Massachusetts he sends Margaret a letter confessing he's been standing her up on their mental dates. "I own with sorrow that much business hath made me too often forget Mondays and Fridays," he wrote.

His earliest American journal entries are understandably brief. "Monday we kept a court," reads one. "My son, Henry Winthrop, was drowned at Salem," says another.

I read somewhere that remnants of the postholes from the Great House are visible in Charlestown. Turns out that's only true if it isn't snowing. Just across the Charlestown Bridge from Boston, the postholes, along with stones from the Three Cranes Tavern built on the site after the Great House was dismantled, are on view in lovely little City Square

Park. The British burned down the tavern during the Battle of Bunker Hill in 1775. I can almost make out the intertwined foundations of the two buildings outlined on the ground.

So much history had already happened on this one patch of grass before the Declaration of Independence was even written. Coming from the West, where history, like everything else, is so spread out, and even then it's mostly grubby Indian wars and greedy copper barons with a little Lewis and Clark in between, I never get sick of the way every inch of Boston seems so jam-packed with the important past, how I'll just be walking down the street and see Sam Adams's grave right next to the sidewalk. On the cab ride to see Winthrop's postholes, past the North End with its Old North Church of "One if by land, and two if by sea" fame, my driver told me about the neighborhood's Great Molasses Flood of 1919, when a colossal tank of molasses broke apart and sent a sweet and gooey wave more than ten feet high cresting through town. "People drowned," he said, adding, "That neighborhood still has a lot of rats."

At City Square Park, I use my shoes as snow scrapers so I can read the snowy plaques saying where Winthrop's front door or his wine cellar or kitchen had been. Unfortunately, my shoes are the dumbest possible ballet flats. Uncovering the "Timber Remains from Great House" marker soaks my socks.

This was where Winthrop wrote a letter to his wife on July 16, 1630. He tells her that he's too busy to write but wants her to know that "yet I live." Still, he opens up to her, allowing himself more sorrow over his son's death than that single sentence in his journal records. "We have met with many sad and discomfortable things . . . and the Lord's hand hath been heavy upon myself," he grumbles. Then this: "My son Henry! my son Henry! ah! Poor child!"

Remembering that outburst of pain, I look down at my soggy socks and over at the postholes of Winthrop's house. Then I just stare at Interstate 93 for a while, wondering how someone whose child had died could still believe in God, much less describe Him as "merciful" and "good."

Winthrop actually praises God for his misfortune. He reassures Margaret he doesn't regret coming, tells her not to worry about her impending voyage the following summer. "My most sweet wife," he coos, "be not disheartened."

How could she not be, though? In September, Winthrop would write Margaret a letter announcing, "Lady Arbella is dead. . . . Thus the Lord is pleased still to humble us. . . . He is our God, and may dispose of us as he sees good." Dispose— what an encouraging word to use around the poor woman he is trying to coax into making a transatlantic death trip. She'll go all that way only to be thrown away like Jehovah's trash.

Within a month, Winthrop records in his journal that Lady Arbella's husband, Isaac Johnson, also "died in sweet peace." Thus the two Massachusetts settlers of the most noble birth were gone by autumn.

In the first year of settlement, the letters home were frequently grim epistles. Deputy Governor Thomas Dudley wrote to the Countess of Lincoln (the late Lady Arbella's mother), "We yet enjoy little to be envied, but endure much to be pitied in the sickness and mortality of our people. . . . There is not [one] house where there is not one dead." As for reinforcements from England, only the well-off need apply. Dudley, perhaps thinking sarcastically of the optimistic Massachusetts seal, writes, "If there be any endowed with grace and furnished with means to feed themselves and theirs for eighteen months, and to build and plant, let them come over into our Macedonia and help us."

The September 30 entry of Winthrop's journal is historic if not exactly illustrious. Winthrop mentions Boston for the very first time, noting that a goat died there.

Winthrop himself is mum on when or why he and his cronies decamped Charlestown for good and made Boston their new home. Edward Johnson, a woodworker who would go on to be one of the founders of the town of Woburn, later recalled that the reason Winthrop and his shipmates traded in Charlestown for Boston "was the want of fresh water." Charlestown had "but one spring," accessible only "when the tide was down."

Go to 276 Washington Street in Boston and see how Winthrop's luck would change by moving there. At that address, on the side of the Winthrop Building, the aforementioned first skyscraper in Boston, there are two plaques. One brags that it was the former "site of the home of the city's first colonial governor, John Winthrop." The other reads, "Here was the Great Spring which for more than two centuries gave water to the people of Boston." Thus did the governor, having learned from his Charlestown mistake, build his house next to the best spring in town.

The original white settler of Boston, then called Shamut, was Englishman William Blaxton (or Blackstone). He invited Winthrop and friends to join him across the Charles River. He had attended Cambridge University with Isaac Johnson and moved to land that is now Boston Common and Beacon Hill in 1625 after he jumped ship from an expedition. He built his little hermit cabin in what is now Louisburg Square, one of the fanciest addresses in town. (Louisa May Alcott lived and died there, and Senator John Kerry, a Winthrop descendant, lives there now.) So Blaxton welcomed the Puritans to join him. Apparently, he enjoyed their company so much that he soon moved to Rhode Island.

John Winthrop writes his wife his first letter marked "Boston in Massachusetts" on November 29, 1630. In it, he cautions her to "provide well for the sea." Goodly portions of the letters he sends Margaret and his son John Jr. before they join him in Massachusetts consist of the same sort of grocery lists Winthrop made before he left. Bring axes, linen, and "a large frying pan," he commands Margaret in one letter. He harangues John Jr. to amass peas and oatmeal ("as much as you can"), "sugar and fruit, pepper and ginger," goats, sheep, garlic, and onions. Winthrop advises him to pack these things in good barrels. After all, he sighs, "We have lost much by bad casks."

Winthrop's last journal entry for 1630 tells the harrowing story of Richard Garrett, a Boston shoemaker he knows from church. Garrett, his daughter, and five others went to Plymouth in a small boat "against the advice of his friends." A windstorm blew them out to sea. Finally, they saw land and made their way to shore. But the wind had splashed so much water into their boat that "some had their legs frozen into the ice, so as they were forced to be cut out." They tried to build a fire, but "having no hatchet, they could get little wood, and were forced to lie in the open air all night, being extremely cold." (Seriously, Margaret, don't forget that ax.) Come morning, two who could walk set out for Plymouth and met a couple of Indian women who had their husbands bring the pair of Bostonians "back to their wigwam, and entertained them kindly." The Indians then guided the two to Plymouth, where the authorities there sent out the seventeenth-century equivalent of a team of first responders, who tried to rescue the freezing others. Still, Garrett died two days later, "the ground being so frozen . . . they could not dig his grave." One of the Indians covered "the corpse" with "a great heap of wood to keep it from the wolves." Three more of them died, including one, wrote Thomas Dudley, who "rotted from the feet upwards where the frost had gotten most hold."

That first winter, living in a town where goats and people die, one of them by rotting "from the feet upwards," Winthrop's sermon about how the colonists would build some fancy city on a hill must have seemed, in retrospect, a tad laughable.

For six glorious weeks in 1999, CBS aired a sitcom with that very premise, in which an idealistic Puritan family called the Winthrops suffered through their grim first winter in colonial Massachusetts. It was called *Thanks.* As in Thanksgiving. As in *thanks a lot.* The show was quickly canceled, but I cannot overstate how excited I was about it. I felt the way an avid stamp collector might if she found out CBS was about to debut its new series, *CSI: Philately.*

As the pilot begins, it's morning. Mrs. Winthrop yells at the children to get out of bed because their "boiling water's ready." Replies her son, "Water! Can I lick the spoon?"

The show's ongoing gag was how miserable all the settlers were—how hungry, how cold, how cramped. The Winthrop daughter, Abigail, was a typical sitcom teenage bombshell daughter. After a disagreement with her parents about boys, she lets loose the sort of routine girl outburst that's been seen on prime time since the dawn of *Gidget.* "I hate my life!" she yells. But where a modern TV teenager would run upstairs and slam the door to her room, the seventeenth-century teenager, living in a tiny one-room cabin, can only run about a foot and a half before she throws herself face first onto a bed right next to the table where everyone would eat, if there was any food.

The main character, here named James Winthrop, though

he's clearly modeled after John, is the lone dreamer in a town full of whiners. He welcomes in the spring, saying, "What a beautiful day it is. The snow is melting. Everyone out and about airing out their clothes, lugging out their dead."

On *Thanks,* the optimism behind the image of the city on a hill was literally a joke. Says the Winthrop stand-in, "We're not the kind of people who are easily discouraged by a few snow flurries, a couple of head colds, the fifty-percent mortality rate." No, he says, they're "strong-willed people who never give up."

John Winthrop's first journal entry in January 1631 notes that "a house at Dorchester was burnt down." The next entry, in February, states that a Mr. Freeman's house in Watertown burned down but "being in the daytime, his goods were saved." It speaks of the grind of ongoing misery that Winthrop sees a daytime blaze as a sign that things are looking up. Of course he was unaware that he would spend the next few years trying to put out fires of a different sort.

Enter Roger Williams. On February 5, 1631, Winthrop's journal notes the arrival of the ship *Lyon.* "She brought Mr. Williams, (a godly minister), with his wife."

Williams was probably twenty-seven years old. A London-raised, Cambridge-educated theologian, he had most recently worked in Essex as a private chaplain to the family of one of Oliver Cromwell's cousins.

When Williams next appears in Winthrop's journal, two months later, the governor is all riled up. He says that the Boston court (which he runs) wrote a letter to John Endecott, asking him to explain why the Salem church just offered to hire Williams as its teacher.

The bigger Puritan churches employ two equally important clergymen, a pastor and a teacher. Influenced by John Calvin's notion of a fourfold division of church offices (ordained pastor and teacher, lay elders and deacons), the Cambridge Platform of 1648, a sort of manifesto about church organization written by a committee of New England divines, described the difference between the job descriptions: "The pastor's special work is to attend to exhortation, and therein to administer a word of wisdom; the teacher is to attend to doctrine and therein to administer a word of knowledge." The two work side by side, the teacher delivering brainy lectures about Scripture, the pastor giving earthier, encouraging talks about living a devout daily life. (For instance, Cotton Mather described Samuel Newman, the pastor at Dorchester and Weymouth, as "a very lively preacher, and a very preaching liver.") If the pastor is the church's heart, the teacher is its brain. John Cotton, the future teacher at Boston, sounds like a fervent researcher when he describes his own "love to the truth, which is to be searched after more than hidden treasure." It makes sense that Williams would be offered the job of teacher—he cares more about searching for the truth than making friends, his ideas outnumbering his social skills.

Both teacher and pastor are elected positions. The members of each congregation choose their own clergy. There is no difference between Puritan clergymen and Anglican priests in terms of authority and the respect and obedience worshippers are supposed to have for that authority. A Puritan teacher or pastor, like a priest, is supposed to guide the worshippers in spiritual life and study. The difference between Puritan clergy and Anglican priests is how they are chosen—a priest from the top down (the top being the Archbishop of Canterbury) and a teacher from the bottom up (that being the congregation). Each congregation in New England is to be its own autonomous authority.

When Winthrop and the other Boston settlers formed their church the previous August, they had chosen John Wilson as their teacher. Wilson, however, was sailing back to England on the *Lyon*'s return trip to retrieve his wife. This is a setback for the Boston church. Winthrop admires Wilson, calling him "a very sincere, holy man." Winthrop writes approvingly in his journal that Wilson confessed that before coming to Massachusetts, he dreamed "that he saw a church arise out of the earth, which grew up and became a marvelous goodly church." It's clear Winthrop wants to make sure Wilson's dream comes true. With Wilson's leave of absence upon them, Winthrop pens a sad little entry about holding a prayer meeting in his home at which Wilson encourages Winthrop and Dudley to preach lay sermons while he's gone.

The fact that Williams, a minister, came in on the very

ship that was to sail away with Boston's minister must have seemed pretty much perfect, as if heaven's Human Resources Department had sent Williams their way. However, they would soon suspect that Roger Williams was the preacher from hell.

Winthrop notes that in the letter the Boston court sent to Endecott in Salem, "Mr. Williams had refused to join with the congregation at Boston, because they would not make a public declaration of their repentance for having communion with the churches of England, while they lived there." In other words, the congregation of Boston, people whose faith led them to Massachusetts, people who had somehow survived that first, grim winter with all its hardships and loss, are being told by some upstart new guy that they haven't done enough for their God, that they are damned until the entire congregation publicly apologizes for having ever worshipped in Church of England churches back in England. These Nonseparatists still consider themselves to be members of the Church of England, reformers trying to set a new example and fix the church from within. In fact, when the Bostonians chose Wilson as their teacher the previous summer, Winthrop writes in his journal as if the Archbishop of Canterbury is looking over his shoulder, confirming that the teacher's election does not mean that "Mr. Wilson should renounce his ministry he received in England."

To Williams, the Bay colonists' way of walking the Separatist walk while refusing to talk the Separatist talk was hypocrisy. But besides being a survival tactic meant to keep them in the good graces of King Charles, Boston's insistence on maintaining its ties and affection for their brethren back in England is also compassionate. Giles Firmin, a onetime deacon of the Boston church, in his 1652 tract *Separatism Examined,* explained, "When I raise a house new from the ground, I may then do as I please, but if I be mending an old house, I must do as well as I can, repair by degrees."

So after the Boston church is kind enough to extend an offer to Roger Williams to fill one of the roughly two paying church job openings in all of New England, Williams would later recall, "I conscientiously refused . . . because I durst not officiate to an unseparated people, as, upon examination and conference, I found them to be."

If Roger Williams had any ambition at all, he would have accepted the Bostonians' offer on the spot with, if not hugs and giggles, then whatever modicum of humble joy a Puritan is allowed. The position of teacher in Boston is the most plum appointment in seventeenth-century New England theology. When the already famous go-getter John Cotton arrives in Boston two years later, he will assume that position until his death and in doing so he goes down in history as the most important and influential clergyman of the era.

Roger Williams might be the most ambitious of all the New England Puritans, but his ambitions are strictly spiritual. He fears no man, only God. He desires heavenly riches, not earthly influence. He seeks absolute communion with his Creator and he does not in 1631, nor will he ever, care about anything more. His fellow New Englanders find his zeal kind of inspirational but awfully off-putting.

So from the get-go Roger Williams comes off as a fully formed crank, a man whom even Puritans dismiss as a tad too fanatical. By turning down the Boston teacher job, he is nitpicky, annoying, galling, and rude. But he is nevertheless principled, self-confident, forthright, and true to himself. In this earliest run-in, he also makes a small, preliminary stand that hints at his later legacy of calling for the separation of church and state. Along with rebuffing the Bostonians' job offer, Williams informs Winthrop and his fellow magistrates that, by the way, they have no right (records Winthrop) "to punish breach of the Sabbath, nor . . . any other breach of the first table."

The first table is the first four of the Ten Commandments, the ones having to do with God—not worshipping another god, not making idols, not taking the Lord's name in vain, and keeping the Sabbath holy. Keeping the Sabbath holy is Massachusetts Bay law and therefore punishable by the General Court. Williams believes that adhering to the first four commandments is a religious matter and not the business of civil magistrates. Williams makes a distinction between a sin and a crime.

Getting wind of this, the civil magistrates must have screamed a collective "Goddamnit!" Or would have but for Commandment Three. Threatening to take away a Puritan magistrate's right to punish is like yanking the trumpet out of Louis Armstrong's hands. As Williams will soon find out, punishment is what the General Court is *for.* Winthrop erupts, and not only at Williams. He's just as upset with Endecott's church in Salem. How dare they elect Williams as their teacher after that troublemaker insulted Boston's church and magistrates?

When Endecott receives the court's scolding letter, the Salem church withdraws its job offer to Williams, so Williams heads to Separatist Plymouth, where he will stay until he realizes even Plymouth is not quite Separatist enough. Plymouth's Governor Bradford calls Williams "a man godly and zealous . . . but very unsettled in judgment." Bradford says that when Williams "exercised his gifts among us," his teaching was "well-approved." Bradford blesses God for sending Williams to him and even claims to be "thankful to [Williams] even for his sharpest admonitions and reproofs, so far as they agree with the truth." His point being, a lot of Williams's reprimands were full of crap. Williams, said Bradford, "fell into some strange opinions . . . which caused some controversy between the church and him."

One of these strange opinions involved Williams reprimanding Plymouth residents who, when visiting friends and family back in England, would go to church with them—Church of England church. If a godly American so much as accompanied his elderly English mother to tea with her vicar, Williams had a fit, bemoaning those who profess "to be a separate people in New England . . . and yet communicating with the parishes in Old." So Williams departs Plymouth "abruptly," says Bradford, and returns once again to Salem, a town not immune to strange opinions.

Roger Williams is hardly the only argumentative Jesus freak within John Winthrop's jurisdiction. Winthrop's problem with Williams isn't so much that he says strange things, it's that Williams persists in believing strange things after he has been shown the errors of his ways. Winthrop's journal is chockablock with grievances to mediate and wrongheaded people to set straight. There's no agreeing to disagree in Massachusetts Bay. There is only agreeing to agree. Winthrop's perpetual task is consensus-building.

For example, it seems the Watertown pastor has been telling his flock that "the churches of Rome were true churches." Wrong! So Winthrop, along with Deputy Governor Thomas Dudley and a Boston church elder, hurries to Watertown to organize a debate before the congregation and the pastor. Perhaps Winthrop whips out that Geneva Bible with its marginal note in the Book of Revelation about the pope being the Whore of Babylon. Can a true church have the Whore of Babylon in charge—can it really? Luckily, everyone in the congregation "except three" admits his error and all's well. (Then, later on, one of the dissenters will be excommunicated for a few hours until he finally concedes he's mistaken and is un-excommunicated and welcomed back into the fold and all is well yet again.)

On November 2, 1631, Margaret Winthrop, along with John Jr., arrives, prompting something of a town party in Boston. Winthrop writes that the "assistants and most of the people . . . came to welcome them," bringing hogs and poultry, venison and geese, "so as the like joy and manifestation of love had never been seen in New England." This outpouring of foodstuffs and goodwill must have convinced Margaret that she had married Mr. Popularity. She'll soon discover that her husband will need an ally at home more than ever, as he has a nemesis at work.

If Nancy Drew were trying to get to the bottom of Winthrop's petty rivalry with Deputy Governor Thomas Dudley, the book might be titled *The Mystery of the Pretentious Wainscoting*. What happened was, the assistants had agreed to build a fortified new town across the Charles River from Boston, which, per New England's usual creativity with naming things, they called "New Town." (It would eventually be renamed Cambridge, after they founded a university there. Because what else would men who attended England's Cambridge University name a university town?) So Winthrop and Dudley started building houses there. Then Winthrop's Boston neighbors cajoled the governor not to abandon them, and so he promised "he would not leave them." When Winthrop has his servants start dismantling his New Town house, Dudley is miffed. So Dudley quits his post as deputy governor in a huff. Which was, notes Winthrop in his journal, "not allowed."

Following a meeting on May 1, 1632, Winthrop writes

that Dudley defends his resignation as a gesture of keeping the "public peace," that when he airs his hurt feelings "he saw that bred disturbance." Supposedly, the purpose of the meeting is for everyone to kiss and make up. But the Winthrop of "Christian Charity," the one who admonished that "the rich and mighty should not eat up the poor," presses Dudley on why he just sold some corn to poor people at too steep a price. "There arose hot words," writes Winthrop, who continues, "The governor"—Winthrop frequently refers to himself in the third person—"took notice of these speeches, and bore them with more patience than he had done." Then, in another dumb diplomatic move, given how sensitive Dudley is on the subject of new houses in New Town, Winthrop slams Dudley for building a fancy mansion there, unseemly "in the beginning of a plantation." Winthrop's complaint? Adorning the house with ostentatious wainscoting. Doesn't Winthrop realize that part of "rejoicing together," as he put it in "Model of Christian Charity," is complimenting one another's wood paneling? Dudley is surely offended and protests that his wainscoting "was for the warmth of his house . . . being but clapboards nailed to the wall in the form of wainscot."

A week later, Winthrop would be reelected governor and Dudley "accepted his place again" as deputy. At which time Winthrop enthuses, "The governor and he being reconciled the day before, all things were carried very lovingly." But by August, Dudley was complaining about Winthrop's abandonment of New Town again, and questioning Winthrop's authority and decisions. This is when Dudley levels that charge about letting Philip Ratcliffe hang around too long after being banished the previous winter. Dudley also accuses Winthrop of lending twenty-eight pounds of gunpowder to Plymouth during some Indian troubles without the court's consent. Winthrop writes, "The Governor answered, it was of his own powder."

Winthrop sat there calmly, lapping up the insults dished out by Dudley. To his journal he explains his approach to Dudley this way: "To clear his reputation with those to whom the deputy had accused him, he was willing to give him satisfaction . . . that he might free him of such jealousy." Nice try.

These are, after all, Englishmen, a people with such a knack for infighting that the coming decade carries their countrymen back home into civil war. Throughout the 1630s, Winthrop's journal documents a Massachusetts Bay always on the brink of arguing itself into oblivion. The body politic constantly threatens to kill itself, and Winthrop is the guy who puts in a lot of late nights manning the suicide hotline.

Just as Watertown got the crackdown for kind thoughts about the Catholic Church and thus not being puritanical enough, Winthrop also has to rein in those Puritans he fears will purify the colony to pieces. Case in point, the uproar over the red cross on the king's flag.

It might seem strange that such a gung-ho group of Christians would abhor the symbol of the cross, the very wooden structure that makes possible their savior's sacrifice. But the Puritans think of the cross as a graven image that therefore breaks the Second Commandment against idol worship. A cross, to a Puritan, is not a symbol of Christ—it is a symbol of the pope. In his journal Winthrop notes that once, coming home to Boston after a visit to Plymouth, he "came to a place called Hue's Cross." He continues, "The governor being displeased at the name" because it might "give the Papists occasion to say that their religion was first planted in these parts, changed the name, and called it Hue's Folly."

As for the flag controversy, one day in 1634, a certain Salem resident who shall remain John Endecott, noticed the king's flag with its red cross of Saint George whipping in the wind. So he ordered the cross to be cut out of the flag. In his journal, Winthrop is conflicted. On the one hand, Endecott has a point: "the red cross was given to the king of England by the pope, as an ensign of victory, and so a superstitious thing, and a relic of antichrist." (He is referring to the Crusades, when the red cross of Saint George was England's pope-approved battle flag.) On the other hand, if news of this got back to England, "it would be taken as an act of rebellion . . . in defacing the king's colors."

In a later entry, Winthrop describes hosting a powwow of the assistants at his house. They know that gossip this juicy is not going to stay on this side of the Atlantic for long, so they agree to appease the king by writing an open letter to Winthrop's brother-in-law in England, telling "the truth of the matter . . . therein we expressed our dislike of the thing, and our purpose to punish the offenders."

Eventually the court condemns Endecott, according to Winthrop, not so much for defacing the flag, but for acting "rash" and on his own, for "not seeking the advice of the court." They find Endecott "uncharitable," making a unilateral decision for Salem that the officers of the General Court had a right to discuss and debate and come to a collective agreement about. Endecott is also taken to task for "laying a blemish also upon the rest of the magistrates, as if they would suffer idolatry . . . and giving occasion to the state of England to think ill of us." I.e., Endecott made the court look sloppy, as if it had been oblivious to an idol of popery in its midst. Endecott is censured from holding public office for a year, receiving this mild sentence and not, say, having his ears sliced off with his own flag-ripping sword, because he acted "out of tenderness of conscience, and not any evil intent." In other words, they agreed with what he did, just not the showboating way he did it.

Winthrop is wise to fear the king's wrath. For starters, a few of the men Winthrop and his court had banished back to England, including the earless Philip Ratcliffe—who, for some reason, holds a grudge—were stirring up trouble against the colony, petitioning the king to the effect that Massachusetts Bay is set on "rebellion, to have cast off our allegiance, and to be wholly separate from the church and laws of England." They also complained that the "ministers and people" of Massachusetts "did continually rail against the state, church, and bishops there."

Of course, there was plenty of railing against the state and especially against the bishops, going on back in England, too; especially against Bishop Laud, King Charles's closest ally in the clergy, whom Charles would officially appoint Archbishop of Canterbury in 1633. Laud is as firm a believer in the Church of England as the Puritans are firm in their beliefs. Which is highly, severely, vindictively, insanely firm. Laud's rather understandable problem with Calvinism's harsh insistence on predestination made him proclaim, "My very soul abominates this doctrine, for it makes God, the God of all mercies, to be the most fierce and unreasonable tyrant in the whole world." An excellent point. Yet how does the highest authority in the Church of England choose to counter the Puritans for having turned God into a tyrant? With unfettered tyranny, of course.

Laud oversaw a network of informants around England whose job it was to report Anglican ministers who slacked off in providing their parishioners with the finer things—the organ music, the vestments, the candles, and kneeling—that sickened Puritan-leaning clergymen. Trespassing preachers were hauled before Laud's Court of High Commission, and if they failed to repent they were thrown in jail.

In 1633, a friend warned John Cotton that just such a letter demanding he appear before Laud's commission was on its way to him. According to his grandson Cotton Mather, Cotton's friend broke it to him "that if he had been guilty of drunkenness, or uncleanness, or any such lesser fault, he could have obtained his pardon; but inasmuch as he had been guilty of . . . puritanism, the crime was unpardonable; and therefore, said he, you must fly for your safety." So Cotton went into hiding. He was forty-eight, he was venerable, and he was on the lam. He found refuge in the houses of other like-minded ministers and friends, but wrote his wife, Sarah, not to visit him because "I fear you will be watched, and dogged at the heels. But I hope, shortly God will make way for thy safe coming."

Hearing of Cotton's predicament, John Winthrop invited him to Boston. And on September 4, 1633, Winthrop's journal notes Cotton's arrival, along with Puritan firebrand Thomas Hooker, on the ship *Griffin.* "They gat out of England with much difficulty," writes Winthrop, Cotton and Hooker both having been "long sought for to have been brought into the high commission." Their fellow minister Thomas Shepard, who would soon follow them to America, remarked, "I saw the Lord departing from England when Mr. Hooker and Mr. Cotton were gone."

The Boston congregation reassigned John Wilson as their pastor and elected Cotton their teacher. (The studious Cotton would later justify escaping to America to avoid prison in London, "where there would be no opportunity for books or pens.") Cotton's preaching was a big hit. Within three months, Winthrop remarks in his journal, many "profane and notorious evil persons came and confessed their sins, and were comfortably received into the bosom of the church" in Boston.

John Cotton arrives in 1633 just in time to help Massachusetts Bay board up its theological windows. Hurricane Roger is a coming. Winthrop reports in his journal that he turns to Cotton for advice. It seems Roger Williams has arrived at some exciting new conclusions, which he has generously decided to share with his fellow colonists.

Neither Williams nor Cotton will ever get over their arguments of 1633–35. The two will spend the rest of their lives irking each other so much they would engage in the seventeenth-century New England version of a duel: pamphlet fight! Since the contemporary record of Massachusetts Bay's quarrel with Williams, and vice versa, consists mostly of Winthrop's journal, Williams and Cotton's later publications are handy for getting the skinny on what the original fuss was about. Williams publishes "Letter of Mr. John Cotton," unbeknownst to its sender; then Williams publishes his own rebuttal, "Mr. Cotton's Letter Examined and Answered." Cotton then publishes "John Cotton's Answer to Roger Williams." After which Williams publishes a pamphlet taking Cotton to task, *The Bloudy Tenent of Persecution.* Then Cotton slams Williams right back with *The Bloudy Tenent Washed and Made White in the Blood of the Lamb.* Then Williams counterattacks with *The Bloudy Tenent Yet More Bloudy.* Only death prevented Cotton from finishing his final sequel, *The Bloudy Tenent: Attack of the Clones.*

On December 27, 1633, Winthrop writes in his journal that he has met with the court of assistants and some of "the most judicious ministers," which would include Cotton, about a "treatise" Williams sent to the governor of Plymouth "wherein, among other things, he disputes their right to the lands they possessed here, and concluded that, claiming by the king's grant, they could have no title, nor otherwise, except they compounded with the natives." In other words, Williams says the royal charter that gave Plymouth the rights to Plymouth is illegal because what Plymouth really needed was a deed from the Indians. Williams is under the impression the land belonged to its original inhabitants.

Winthrop continues that the magistrates and the ministers are also "much offended" by Williams's description of the late King James as a liar who committed the blasphemy of "calling Europe Christendom, or the Christian world."

Roger Williams is God's own goalie—no seemingly harmless pleasantry gets past him. To Williams, "Christendom," that affable word describing Europe and its colonies, is an affront to Christ. For this, he blames Constantine the Great.

Is he referring to Constantine, the first Roman emperor to legalize Christianity in the year 313, thereby allowing Christians to worship in peace after centuries in the Coliseum as lion food? Yep, that's the jerk.

In *The Bloudy Tenent,* Williams points out that Constantine "did more to hurt Christ Jesus than the raging fury of the most bloody Neroes." At least under the Christian persecutor

Nero, who was rumored to have had the Apostle Paul beheaded and Saint Peter crucified upside down, Christianity
was a pure (if hazardous) way of life. But when Constantine
himself converted to Christianity, that's when the Church was
corrupted and perverted by the state. Williams explains that
under Constantine, "the gardens of Christ's churches turned
into the wilderness of national religion, and the world (under
Constantine's dominion) to the most unchristian Christendom." Legalizing, legitimizing the Church turned Christianity
into just another branch of government enforced by "the
sword of civil power," i.e., through state-sponsored violence.

On the one hand, there is no surer sign that Williams
should probably ease up his Christian truth quest than when
the magistrates of Massachusetts Bay find him to be too
theologically intense. I just feel sorry for him that he lived in
an age before air quotes; maybe he would have calmed down
about use of the word "Christendom" if he could make sarcastic hand gestures every time he heard or said it.

On the other hand, Williams makes an interesting point.
Remember that Christendom, at the moment he complains
about King James once using that word on a charter, is at war
with itself, that being the Thirty Years' War. Catholics are
slaughtering Protestants in France and Protestants are
slaughtering Catholics in Germany. A year after Williams arrived in Boston, the town held a day of Thanksgiving to celebrate the fall of Munich at the hands of Gustavus Adolphus,
Sweden's Protestant king. Williams would later write, "The

blood of so many hundred thousand souls of Protestants and Papists, spilt in the wars of present and former ages, for their respective consciences, is not required nor accepted by Jesus Christ the Prince of Peace."

Winthrop issues a warning to John Endecott in Salem, where Williams was living, pointing out that Williams's treasonous put-downs are not confined to the late king but include the current one. Winthrop alludes to Williams citing three particularly mean verses from the Book of Revelation that he "did personally apply to our present king, Charles."

Williams backs down—for now. He writes "very submissively" to Winthrop and the council that he regrets the hubbub and permits his treatise "to be burnt." A few weeks later, Winthrop is pleased to report that the Reverends Cotton and Wilson were mollified by Williams's "retraction."

In May of 1634, Winthrop writes in his journal, "The court chose a new governor, viz., Thomas Dudley, Esq., the former deputy." Winthrop is elected deputy governer. In other words, he is now his rival's number two. He is surely embarrassed but his diary contains no bellyaching. It was of course God's will, so he deserved it. In fact, Winthrop has all the assistants over for dinner. Though, perhaps to cheer himself up about his accomplishments while governor, he does write a letter to a friend in England a few days later talking up the colony's improved mortality stats. "There hath not died above two or three grown persons and about so many children all the last year," he boasts.

In July of 1634, the assistants receive a letter from Matthew Craddock, the Massachusetts Bay Company's man in England. The Commission for Regulating Plantations, headed by the king's pet, Bishop Laud, is recalling the patent, i.e., the Charter. Craddock "wrote to us to send it home," records Winthrop. Ship back the Charter and they might as well pack up the whole colony in the same trunk. The assistants agree to reply to Craddock's letter, but without the Charter, and without "any answer or excuse." Poor Craddock—ordered by Laud to procure a document and all he gets in return is a letter about how the weather sure is hot in Boston? Winthrop records that Craddock fires back, enclosing in his reply, hint-hint, a copy of the government order "whereby we were required to send over our patent." Unnerved, the assistants nevertheless write Craddock back that they couldn't possibly legally return the Charter to England "but by a general court," which would not be held until the following September.

In Winthrop's next entry, the assistants meet on Castle Island in Boston Harbor where they conspire to build a fort. Remember the apocalyptic paranoia that inspired the passengers on the Winthrop fleet to quit England in the first place? Well, that was mostly superstitious conjecture based on pessimistic readings of biblical prophets and worries that the Thirty Years War might spread to England. This business of the king's committee recalling the charter is an actual concrete threat to their hard-won way of life. Winthrop was born the year his country's fleet defeated the mighty Spanish Armada; he knows English monarchs are not shy about dispatching their battleships when provoked.

In August, Winthrop gets word that the colony's enemies in England, led by men banished from Massachusetts, have made "railing speeches and threats against this plantation and Mr. Winthrop in particular." They succeeded in getting Laud's committee to appoint a governor to come to Massachusetts with a military escort and take over. By January, Winthrop says, the assistants and ministers hold a meeting in Boston to discuss "what we ought to do, if a general governor should be sent out of England."

In his journal, Winthrop records their answer to that cataclysmic question of how the men of Massachusetts should respond to the arrival of a royal interloper sent to put an end to their city on a hill: "We ought not to accept him."

Remember this is almost a century and a half before the Boston Tea Party, before Lexington and Concord, before the Battle of Bunker Hill in Charlestown burns down that tavern built on the site of Winthrop's first American house. John Winthrop is no Son of Liberty. He's a Puritan father of communal control. But behind the politeness of that line, "We ought not to accept him," Winthrop reveals himself. He is a pussy-footing pragmatist who will clap his own hand over Roger Williams's mouth and confiscate John Endecott's sword if it keeps from riling up King Charles. But we know from Winthrop's journal that he left England with a recipe for gunpowder. That same journal is clear about this: if the king's men come for Massachusetts, Massachusetts will be ready.

Where do these men get such cheek? They are the king's subjects, not citizens. What are the sources of their defiance? There are, I think, primarily two: the Bible and the Magna Carta.

The Bible is full of anecdotes that prime the pump of treason. We have already read of King James's irritation with the way the Geneva Bible's marginal notes spell out how it is biblically sanctioned to defy the Egyptian pharaoh (and therefore all monarchs) when he commands that Hebrew babies be murdered. But those prickly Protestant marginal notes are simply amplifying what's already in the text. I grew up on the King James Version of the Bible, the translation that was, by definition, supposed to be more tolerable to kings, and I would like to point out that by the time I was eight I had already put on a puppet show about how people of faith are required to stand up to wrongheaded kings.

Every summer when I was a kid I attended vacation Bible school. It was like arts-and-crafts camp, only churchier—firing and glazing ceramic praying-hands bookends, that sort of thing. We studied the Book of Daniel's third chapter, in which Nebuchadnezzar, the king of Babylon, commissioned a gold idol that his subjects were required to bow down to. Anyone failing to kneel before the image "shall be cast into the midst of a burning fiery furnace." Kneeling before a false idol being an obvious violation of the Second Commandment, three Jews on Nebuchadnezzar's payroll refuse to worship another god. The three lawbreakers, Shadrach, Meshach, and Abednego, are hauled before the king, who tells them that when he said that thing about the fiery furnace he really meant it. They reply that perhaps God will save them from the flames, "But if not, be it known unto thee, O king, that we will not serve thy gods, nor worship the golden image which thou hast set up."

Those words are insolent and bold, even when spoken by a felt puppet with glued-on googly eyes. The three hope God will save them, but if not they will gladly burn. Nebuchadnezzar is happy to help them find out. He has Shadrach, Meshach, and Abednego thrown into the furnace. To mimic the flames, my fellow Bible students and I rattled flashlights at the puppets, who remained perfectly still and perfectly unharmed, not a yarn hair on their heads singed. "They have no hurt," marveled the king, who decreed that anyone from anywhere who spoke against "the God of Shadrach, Meshach, and Abednego, shall be cut in pieces, and their houses shall be made a dunghill: because there is no other God that can deliver after this sort." A happy ending—the faithful defy the king and the king admits he was wrong.

The lessons of that story—be true to yourself, be not afraid to defy authority, be willing to die for what you believe in—had a profound influence on my own moral backbone, and I am not alone. In his "Letter from the Birmingham Jail," Martin Luther King, Jr., writes of the lawbreaking that landed him in the clink: "Of course, there is nothing new about this kind of civil disobedience. It was evidenced sublimely in the refusal of Shadrach, Meshach and Abednego to obey the laws of Nebuchadnezzar, on the ground that a higher moral law was at stake."

In 1940, when more than 300,000 British and French troops were trapped on the beach in the Belgian coastal town of Dunkirk, awaiting certain death at the hands of the approaching German army, the British commander there sent a three-word message to England of his men's resolve to stick it out and fight: "But if not." Stirred by the subtle reference to Shadrach, Meshach, and Abednego, the British people jumped into their yachts and fishing boats by the thousands and raced across the English Channel to ferry the soldiers to safety.

"God's people have been immovable, constant, and resolved to the death in refusing to submit to false worships, and in preaching and professing the true worship, contrary to the express command of public authority," wrote Roger Williams in *The Bloudy Tenent*. He continued, "So the three famous worthies against the command of Nebuchadnezzar."

Of course a mischief-maker like Williams would make Shadrach, Meshach, and Abednego his personal mascots. But the more mild-mannered Winthrop read the same Bible, including the Geneva Version, where the notes on the Book of Daniel are typically feisty toward royal authority. Perhaps Winthrop, his peripheral vision ever scanning the horizon for the warships of King Charles, perused Daniel 3:19, when

Nebuchadnezzar instructs the furnace operators to crank up the heat "seven times" hotter for his three victims. The Geneva marginal note to that verse reads:

> This declares that the more that tyrants rage, and the more crafty they show themselves in inventing strange and cruel punishments, the more is God glorified by his servants, to whom he gives patience and constancy to abide the cruelty of their punishment.

As for the second source of the New Englanders' impertinence, the Magna Carta, it came about for the same reason so many landmarks of liberty, including the Declaration of Independence, were established in the English-speaking world—because the upper middle class balked at paying taxes. In 1215, armed English barons, sick of being bilked to pay for King John's wars in France, captured London. Seeking a truce, the king met the barons at Runnymede, a meadow by the river Thames, and they hammered out an agreement in Latin that came to be called Magna Carta, the Great Charter.

Many of the Magna Carta's sixty-three clauses enumerate antiquated rules about knights, forests, wine measurement, removing fish-weirs from the Thames, owing money to Jews, and, in case anyone is worried, restoring "the son of Llywelyn and all the hostages from Wales." But two concepts in it stuck. Clause 39 states, "No free man shall be taken or imprisoned or outlawed or exiled or in any way ruined . . . except by the lawful judgment of his peers or by the law of the land." In other words, the king can't just jail his subjects on a whim. Clause 40 declares, "To no one will we sell, to no one will we deny or delay right or justice." In other words, a prisoner cannot be locked up indefinitely without a sentence. Thus the basic gist of the Magna Carta is that no one—including the king—is above the law of the land.

In 1628, two years before the Winthrop fleet sailed for Massachusetts, the Magna Carta was enjoying something of a comeback thanks to the Five Knights Case and the Petition of Right. In 1627, Charles I jailed five Members of Parliament who refused to pay a forced loan to underwrite his war in Spain. Charles, who had held a grudge against Spain ever since the court at Madrid turned down his proposal of marriage to the Spanish princess, had dispatched his armies, under the command of his incompetent best friend, the Duke of Buckingham, to go to war with Spain. Things were not going well. Buckingham's expedition to attack Cadiz in 1625, for example, was pure slapstick—English troops stumbled onto warehouses stocked with Spanish wine and got too drunk to fight. So when five English knights (members of the landed gentry) refused the king's demand of a "loan" (which would probably never be repaid) to fund such foreign-policy buffoonery, Charles had them thrown in jail for who knows how long.

Parliament rallied to the knights' cause, arguing that the Magna Carta denied the king the right to jail his subjects on a whim and forever. Edward Coke, the most important English legal mind of the seventeenth century, led the charge against the king, famously proclaiming to Parliament, "Take heed what we yield unto! Magna Carta is such a fellow that he will have no sovereign." Coke helped author Parliament's landmark response in 1628, the Petition of Right. It states:

> It is declared and enacted, that no freeman may be taken or imprisoned or be disseized of his freehold or liberties, or his free customs, or be outlawed or exiled, or in any manner destroyed, but by the lawful judgment of his peers, or by the law of the land.

(By the way, the confrontational Coke was the mentor and benefactor of that most confrontational of New England colonists, Roger Williams. Coke paid for Williams's education. Williams would later write Coke's daughter that her father's "example, instruction, and encouragement have spurred me on to a more than ordinary, industrious and patient course." Williams might have also picked up his sometimes impenetrable writing style from Coke. Coke's *Institutes of the Laws of England* was still the standard legal textbook more than a century later when Thomas Jefferson went to law school—much to Jefferson's dismay; he complained of Coke, "I am sure I never was so tired of an old dull scoundrel in my life." Once, in one of his many letters to Winthrop, Williams confessed his fear that "my lines are as thick and over busy as mosquitoes.")

Coke and Parliament goaded Charles I into signing off on

the Petition of Right. Of course, Charles pretty much ignored it, and canceled Parliament the following year, prompting some of the jitters that made so many Englishmen, including Winthrop, flee to New England. Nevertheless, the Petition was on the books. Its reframing of the Magna Carta's call for due process, writes Winston Churchill, is "the main foundation of English freedom." He continues, "The right of the Executive Government to imprison a man . . . for reasons of State was denied; and that denial, made good in painful struggles, constitutes the charter of every self-respecting man at any time in any land."

Is this not stirring? Churchill wrote that in his *History of the English-Speaking Peoples,* and every time I read those words I am proud to be an English-speaking person.

All of which to say, those penny-pinching barons at Runnymede, those knights and Coke and Parliament standing up to the crown, made it thinkable for Thomas Dudley, John Winthrop, and the other assistants in Massachusetts Bay Colony's court to build a fort and train militias and construct a beacon to guard against an invasion by their own king.

That said, just because something is thinkable doesn't mean it's doable, much less desirable. The idea of American independence from Britain is a tea not nearly finished steeping. Though the court quietly readies for war, it does its damnedest to crack down on unnecessarily incendiary talk against the king.

Cue Roger Williams. On November 27, 1634, Winthrop's journal notes that the Court of Assistants got word that Williams "had broken his promise to us, in teaching publicly against the king's patent, and our great sin in claiming right thereby to this country."

In fact, Williams was calling it a "national sin" for the colony to claim the right to Indian lands based on the Charter granted them by the king of England. John Cotton later claimed that Williams was agitating in Salem that in order for the colonists to repent of this sin, it was "a national duty to renounce the patent," which Cotton fears would have "subverted the fundamental state and government of the country." Cotton also reported that among Williams's arguments was a repudiation of England's justification for colonization, that the natives were not using the land because they were not cultivating it properly, not raising cattle. According to Cotton, Williams pointed out that the Indians were using the land—not for farming but for hunting. The Indians, Williams said, "burnt up all the underwoods in the country, once or twice a year." This stewardship, he maintained, was not unlike that of English nobles who "possessed great parks, and the king, great forests in England only for their game, and no man might lawfully invade their property."

John Cotton, in a letter to Williams, rolls his eyes at this logic, cracking, "We did not conceive that it is a just title to so vast a continent to make no other improvement of millions of acres in it, but only to burn it up for pastime." Besides, English nobles don't just use their forests for hunting, "but for timber."

It was Cotton, after all, who, in his 1630 farewell sermon to the Winthrop fleet, "God's Promise to His Plantation," proclaimed, "In a vacant soil, he that taketh possession of it, and bestoweth culture and husbandry upon it, his right it is." Upon whose authority? God's, of course, in "the grand charter given to Adam and his posterity." The Massachusetts Bay Charter, therefore, is merely the legal subset of the original patent God granted His very first human creation. Cotton cites Genesis 1:28: "Multiply, and replenish the earth, and subdue it." He continues, "If therefore any son of Adam come and find a place empty, he hath liberty to come, and fill, and subdue the earth there."

The Charter Winthrop and his friends hold dear as the legal mandate for their American rights and property was therefore in jeopardy from two sides—Laud's commission ordering it be returned to London, and some loudmouth in Salem bellowing that the king had no authority to issue a charter in the first place (news of which might egg on Laud all the more).

Five months later, the magistrates summon Williams to explain why he was preaching in Salem that they should not administer an oath to a "wicked" man. Oaths—loyalty oaths to the colony and testimonial oaths before the court—were a sacred tool of justice to the magistrates. Williams argued that an oath is a promise in the eyes of God, and a wicked man making an oath is a violation of the Third Commandment, causing the sinner "to take the name of God in vain." Now, that is what I call creative commandment interpretation.

Let's pause here and try and look past Williams's seemingly teenage behavior—past his tendency toward fussy and
abrasive theological scrutiny, past his loopy Christian navel-
gazing, past his grating inability to make any of the small,
charitable compromises involved in getting along with other
people. Williams's greatness lies in his refusal to keep his
head down in a society that prizes nothing more than harmony and groupthink. He cares more about truth than popularity or respect or personal safety. And while his pursuit of
truth leads him to some eccentric, if not laughable, applica-
tions of the Ten Commandments, his quest also leads him
to some equally eccentric beliefs about racial equality, self-
determination, and religious liberty that good people now
hold dear. In his tormented, lonesome, obsessive, Calvinist
way, he is free. I find him hard to like, but easy to love.

Until scholar Perry Miller took a hard look at Roger Williams in the 1950s, Williams enjoyed a reputation as a sort of
proto–Thomas Jefferson. A Williams biography published in
1940 was entitled *Irrepressible Democrat*. I can see why.
Even though there is no evidence Jefferson ever read any of
Williams's tracts, Williams's writings do occasionally prefig-
ure Jefferson's to an eerie degree. Williams's description of
what he sees as England's crime of stealing American Indians' land as a "national sin" sidles up to Jefferson's line about
"the original sin of slavery" in the United States. In his 1802
letter to Connecticut's Danbury Baptist Association, Jefferson called for a "wall of separation" between church and

state, an oft-mentioned endorsement of the establishment clause in the First Amendment to the Constitution. But Jefferson was not the first person to use that phrase—it was Williams, bemoaning that the state-sponsored church "opened a gap in the hedge or wall of separation between the garden of the church and the wilderness of the world." Williams wanted to rebuild that wall, replant that hedge to keep out the state. Williams wanted to protect believers from their government. So he's not so much the proto-Jefferson as the un-Jefferson, a man who devotes his life to keeping government out of the church—not the other way around.

Still, as an American citizen whose only religion is the freedom of religion, I'm cheered to follow along as Williams exercises his First Amendment rights 156 years before the First Amendment gets ratified. In the United States, the story of the freedom of religion starts, obviously, with religion—with Roger Williams's (and later, Anne Hutchinson's) war of words with the court and clergy of Massachusetts Bay in general and with John Winthrop in particular.

Winthrop and Williams personify not just the conflict between orthodox Massachusetts and what would become madcap Rhode Island, the freewheeling colony Williams is about to found. They personify what would become the fundamental conflict of American life—between public and private, between the body politic and the individual, between we the people and each person's pursuit of happiness. At his city-on-a-hill best, Winthrop is Pete Seeger, gathering a generation around the campfire to sing their shared folk songs. Williams is Bob Dylan plugging in at Newport, making his own noise.

From this end of history, Roger Williams's specific gripes with Winthrop and Co.—denouncing the blasphemy of ungodly persons swearing oaths, taking issue with magistrates prosecuting Sabbath breakers—seem like ridiculous, antiquated quibbles. But Williams's larger project is to guard against any intrusion of the civil sphere into the religious sphere. He's after the thing free people always enjoy, yearn, or fight for; he calls it "soul-liberty."

I n 1635, Williams's surging obsession with his wall of separation between church and state turns him into a bricklayer straight out of Poe—barricading himself into his lonely little garden until no other person gets in, not even his wife. Winthrop's journal notes that one of Williams's half-baked notions du jour is that visible saints should only pray with other confirmed visible saints to the exclusion of all others, even if said others include his wife and child. How did that go over chez Williams? *Sorry, honey, you know I love you guys, but if you want me to say grace over this bowl of mushy corn, you and the kids are going to have to leave the room.* John Cotton later reveals his compassion for poor Mrs. Williams, a woman "of meek and modest spirit" who suffered Williams's "offensive course which occasioned him for a season to withdraw communion in spiritual duties, even from her also."

Once, Roger Williams was away from home and got word his wife was seriously ill. He wrote her a letter, later published as the pamphlet *Experiments in Spiritual Life and Health,* that gives a reader an inkling of what it must have been like to be married to him.

He addresses Mrs. Williams as "My Dearest Love and Companion in This Vale of Tears," a pleasant enough start. "I now send thee that which I know will be sweeter to thee than honey," he writes, "and of more value than if every line and letter were . . . gold and silver." And what is this gift a girl wants more than jewelry? A sermon on proper Christian behavior, of course.

"For as the Lord loveth a cheerful giver," he points out, "so he also [loves] a cheerful preacher."

Flowers would have been nice. Can't go wrong with flowers. Oh, but that's exactly how Williams sees this how-to manual—as a bouquet. "I send thee (though in winter) a handful of flowers made up in a little posy for thy dear self, and our dear children, to look and smell on, when I as the grass of the field shall be gone, and withered," he writes. See? This is better than regular flowers. Regular flowers can't boss her around from the grave. "All my flowers shall be some choice example, or speech of some son or daughter of God, picked out from the garden of the holy Scriptures."

This charming, romantic get-well card includes this recurring image of a repeat sinner: a dog vomiting, then lapping up its own vomit. There is the comforting reminder that Mrs. Williams should regard her bout of the sniffles as a "warning from heaven to make ready for a sudden call to be gone from hence," i.e., as good practice for death. There is the section in which the women sleeping with biblical men try (and fail) to distract their men from devotion to their Creator: "Hence Job in his great passions and cursings could not be brought (no not by his wife) to speak ill of God." Or: "Samson, though carried away first by a Philistine wife, and then by a Philistine whore, yet can he not be carried away so from the God of Israel." There's the part where Williams invites his wife on a sort of weekend getaway "into the valley of the shadow of death," holding hands perhaps as they "view the rotten skulls of so many innumerable thousands of millions of millions of men and women, like ourselves, gone, gone forever from this life."

"Between a loving couple," writes Williams, "it is not easy to keep in the first flame of love . . . although the fire of the truth and sincerity of marriage love never die, or be extinguished." While that statement is in keeping with the not-so-hot-and-bothered sweet nothings of this document, it's worth noting his reference to the "first flame of love." Apparently, there was one once.

The United States is often called a Puritan nation as a lazy way of saying Americans are sexually repressed. Which seems true, because we all read *The Scarlet Letter* in ninth grade. The Puritans were troubled by adultery, and who can blame them? It is, at the very least, a lapse of common courtesy. But the Puritans were actually quite gung-ho about sexual intercourse for married couples because they believed God came up with it. In fact, a handful of colonial New England women successfully sued for divorce on the grounds of impotence, including Anna Lane of Massachusetts Bay, who accused her husband in 1658 of failing to perform "the duties of a husband," a detail not disputed by Mr. Lane. And speaking of marriage, in colonial New England weddings were "a civil thing," civil unions one might say, performed by magistrates, not clergy. Because a wedding wasn't trumped up as the object in life that saves one's soul—that would be God—but rather more like what it actually is, a change in legal status, an errand at the DMV, with cake.

So marital intercourse for Puritans was perfectly permissible and necessary, but every Puritan's heart belonged to Jesus. Spiritual passion is the one area in a Puritan's life in which he or she is allowed out-and-out abandon. We're talking outpourings of ardor bordering on smut.

Even John Winthrop, upstanding pillar of the community, was not above soft-core mash notes addressed to the Lord inspired by the Song of Solomon. "Draw us with the sweetness of thine odors," he asked Jesus, "that we may run after thee, allure us . . . that thou may possess us as thine own . . . in the love of marriage." He continues, "Let us hear that sweet voice of thine, my love, my dove, my undefiled: spread thy skirt over us and cover our deformity, make us sick with thy love: let us sleep in thine arms and awake in thy kingdom."

"God's children," Williams tells his wife, "like true lovers, delight to be private, and fervent with their heavenly father and husband."

Williams's attraction to Jesus inspires him to write the lyrics to hackneyed pop songs, including, "Let Him kiss me with the kisses of his mouth, for his love is better than wine."

Williams in Salem is such a myopic researcher of biblical truth he doesn't care who gets hurt. His intellectual fervor, coupled with a disregard for practical consequences, reminds me of nuclear physicist J. Robert Oppenheimer, running his secret Manhattan Project lab in Los Alamos with single-minded zeal, then quoting the Bhagavad Gita as the first test of his atomic bomb lights up the desert. "Now I am become Death, the destroyer of worlds," he said.

Meanwhile, the Massachusetts Bay General Court and John Winthrop are trying to keep their precarious little world intact. Williams's singular rhetoric has become too disturbing to the public peace.

Williams finds the kind of civic harmony Winthrop strives for to be overrated, a "false peace" that is no measurement of a society's godliness. In *The Bloudy Tenent* he writes that even American Indians and "the wildest pagans keep the peace of their towns or cities, though neither in one nor the other can any man prove a true church of God in these places, and consequently no spiritual and heavenly peace."

Williams goes on to remark that it is the state that is guilty of true disturbance of the peace by inflicting corporeal punishment on people who question the state. He writes, "Such persons only break the city's or kingdom's peace, who cry out for prison and swords against such who cross their judgment or practice in religion."

Williams would concur with Martin Luther King, Jr.'s, assertion in his "Letter from the Birmingham Jail" that "I am not afraid of the word 'tension.'" Williams is up for verbal battles and argumentative civil wars in lieu of physical violence and corporeal punishment.

The tragedy of Williams is that he was born about 350 years too early to pursue his true calling—television punditry. What he needs is his own show on cable news. That's essentially how he acts before the General Court of Massachusetts Bay, as if he and Winthrop and Dudley are squabbling around some big round table on a Sunday-morning show and when they unhook their contact mikes at the end of the broadcast, they'll all go out for a gentlemanly brunch.

Williams will later write that the Massachusetts Puritans' disagreements with him are reminiscent of the very disagreements those Puritans had with the Church back home, disagreements that led them to the extreme measure of emigrating to the New World. He poses the question of how can they expect him to tow their party line when they came here because they were unwilling to do the same for Bishop Laud? Williams points out, "Alas, who knows not what lamentable differences have [they had with] the same ministers of the Church of England," causing them to abandon "their livings, friends, country, life, rather than conform?"

Williams takes this logic a step further, putting his conflict with the settlers of Massachusetts and their conflict with the Church of England within the larger context of the history of Christianity from its beginnings. He points out that the apostles' preaching caused "uproars and tumults wherever they came." When the Protestant Elizabeth I succeeded the Catholic Bloody Mary, Williams notes that Catholics were suddenly out of fashion and out of favor: "The fathers made the children heretics and the children the father."

Williams asserts that disagreement is inherent in religion. The state has jurisdiction over violations against persons and property but not over the soul. He figures that sinners and unbelievers will get more than what's coming to them at world's end, when angels "shall bind them into bundles, and cast them over the everlasting burnings" of hell. But until then, he posits, let's just try not to kill each other:

> God requireth not an uniformity of religion to be inacted
> and enforced in any civil state; which enforced uniformity
> (sooner or later) is the greatest occasion of civil war, rav-
> ishing of conscience, persecution of Christ Jesus in His

servants, and of the hypocrisy and destruction of millions
of souls.

Is it just me, or is this point still worth lingering over? It's
one thing for nonviolent nonbelievers to throw up their
hands at the way the faithful of various religious faiths seem
to come to blows over dogma. But Williams, a diehard zealot,
is unflinching in his recognition that other diehard zealots
are equally set in their ways. And while he would happily—
happily!—harangue any other persons of faith for days on
end about how wrong they are, he does not think they should
be jailed or hit or stabbed or shot for their stupidity, the eter-
nal flames of hell being punishment enough.

Stranger still, Williams does not mean that a civil state
should allow merely all the variations of Christianity, from Catholicism on down. He means that a civil state should permit
all forms of religion, including "the most paganish, Jewish,
Turkish [Islamic] or Antichristian consciences." These forms
of worship should be legal for "all men in all nations and
countries." Not that Williams will be hosting any interfaith
prayer breakfasts. He insists other religions should be "fought
against." It's just that the only weapon used to fight them
should be "the sword of God's spirit, the Word of God."

According to Winthrop's journal, on July 8, 1635, the
court summons Williams to New Town to explain his

"dangerous opinions" to "the magistracy and the churches."
They grill him on the following beliefs: the notion that magistrates "ought not to punish the breach of the first table" of the
Ten Commandments; that oaths should only be administered
to visible saints; that visible saints should not pray with the
unclean, even their own wives and children. The court also
discussed admonishing the church of Salem for once again
calling Williams to be its teacher. Winthrop notes:

> The said opinions were adjudged by all, magistrates and
> ministers, (who were desired to be present,) to be errone-
> ous, and very dangerous, and the calling of him to office,
> at that time, was judged a great contempt of authority. So,
> in fine, time was given to him and the church of Salem to
> consider of these things till the next general court, and
> then either to give satisfaction to the court, or else to ex-
> pect the sentence; it being professedly declared by the
> ministers, (at the request of the court to give their ad-
> vice,) that he who should obstinately maintain such opin-
> ions . . . were to be removed.

There is a lot going on in that passage. For starters, the ul-
timatum, obviously, that unless Williams recants by the next
court he will be banished. Notice they are in no hurry to carry
out this sentence. Williams is not some outsider mope like
Philip Ratcliffe. Williams is one of them, a visible saint (albeit an exasperating one). So they give him the seventeenth-

century equivalent of a time-out to think through his opinions and come around to theirs. As Winthrop put it in "Christian Charity," they remain "knit together in a bond of love."

Notice also that in Winthrop's description of the hearing, when he brings up the presence of the ministers, he makes it clear that they were invited, and that their role is purely advisory. The colonists actually agree with Williams on the separation of church and state—kind of. It's just that Williams wants a wall between them and Winthrop is happy with a wisp of velvet rope. Massachusetts Bay is not a true theocracy in that the colony would not dream of letting the ministers hold office. Winthrop and his shipmates came here to get away from Bishop Laud, not create another one, and Laud's recent attacks on the Charter only confirm that clergymen should not moonlight as magistrates. The assistants make their decision in consultation with the ministers, but the ministers' advice is not legally binding. Cotton and the others act as a human law library, a source for interpreting the Bible's legal instructions. To Williams, however, this liaison means the ministers are dragging the snow-white robes of Christ through the wilderness muck of government; that's probably why Cotton, more than any of his other Boston critics, becomes the object of Williams's lifelong scorn.

Winthrop writes that at the same meeting some Salem residents petitioned the court for the deed to "some land in Marblehead Neck," near their town. The court refuses them because, says Winthrop, "they had chosen Mr. Williams their teacher, while he stood under question of authority, and so offered contempt to the magistrates." On its face, this retaliation is just plain petty. But the court also displays a troubling disregard for one of its own deeply held principles. Namely, that a Congregationalist church is its own authority and therefore is not beholden to magistrates in their own or any other town. It is an abuse of power for the court to strongarm a town because said town's congregation picked its own minister—a congregation choosing its own minister being the definition of a Congregationalist church. Recall that the court had pulled this four years earlier, when Salem first tried to hire Williams. Salem backed down back then, but at some point the townspeople got the nerve to protest. Winthrop notes that the court's decision prompts the Salem church to "write to other churches, to admonish the magistrates of this as a heinous sin." Out of spite, then, the magistrates bar John Endecott and the other Salem men from the next court "until they should give satisfaction about the letter."

According to Winthrop, by the end of August, Roger Williams is so sick he is "not able to speak." It happens. Williams is under a great deal of stress. It's understandable his body would give out and he would lose his voice.

But common sense is hardly the only means to diagnose Williams's illness. The Massachusetts Bay colonists scrutinize every one of life's ups and downs to deduce a message from God. Like that day in 1632 when some people in Watertown watched a mouse fight a snake and win. For me, the moment the mouse kills the snake would be just another gross but engrossing highlight on the Discovery Channel. For them, it is a big, whopping omen. Winthrop happily records the minister John Wilson's interpretation: "That the snake was the devil; the mouse was a poor contemptible people, which God had brought hither, which should overcome Satan here, and dispossess him of his kingdom."

Thus John Cotton later harangues Williams about his post-showdown laryngitis, "When you over-heated yourself in reasoning and disputing against the light of [God's] truth, it pleased him to stop your mouth by a sudden disease, and to threaten to take your breath from you." Get well soon!

M eanwhile, in October 1635, Winthrop's journal marks the arrival in Boston of one of the most endearing and sane men of the seventeenth century, Henry Vane the Younger. Vane will have a long career and meet a sad and unfair end, but wherever he turns up—New England now and the English Parliament later—he is usually a voice of reason, moderation, liberty, and love.

Winthrop describes Vane as "a young gentleman of excellent parts." Harry Vane is hands down the fanciest person yet to set foot in New England, the twenty-three-year-old son of the financial advisor to King Charles. Vane is of such high birth and immense wealth, his decision to cast off the trappings of his background—castle included—and move to this slapdash shantytown at the edge of the world says a lot about his piety. Winthrop, clearly impressed, praises Vane as "being called to the obedience of the gospel, forsook the honors and preferments of the court, to enjoy the ordinances of Christ in their purity here."

To the dismay of his overly Anglican parents, Vane the Younger converted to Puritanism as a teenager and made stops on his postcollegiate tour of Europe in Leiden and Geneva, world capitals of Calvinist thought. When he returned to England, his father asked Bishop Laud himself to talk some sense into the boy, but as one of his father's acquaintances described young Vane in a letter, "No persuasion of our bishops, nor authority of his parents could prevail with him." Kids today! Vane the Elder had hoped the Younger would go into the family business and work for the king instead of ditching his birthright for some ashram in the woods.

In a letter Vane the Younger sent to Vane the Elder before shipping out to Massachusetts, he is keenly aware that his father feels betrayed by his defection. He just hopes his father comes to terms with his decision "before you die," otherwise "the jealousy you have of me would break my heart." "My heart," he writes, "I am sure is sincere, and from hence flows the sweet peace I enjoy with my God amidst these many and heavy trials which now fall upon me." Thinking of the Atlantic crossing ahead, and the unknown wilderness of the New World, Vane reassures his father that this spiritual calm "is my only support in the loss of all other things."

If Harry Vane is on his way to Massachusetts to nurture the sweet peace he enjoys with his God, boy is he in for a surprise. He will spend only two years in New England, but they are the two most turbulent, action-packed years in the history of the Massachusetts Bay Colony. He will witness the havoc wrought by an Indian war and an outspoken female heretic and, at the moment of his autumn landing, the controversy with Roger Williams.

Recall that in the summer of 1635 Williams is laid up sick. He couldn't talk, but he could still write. Come fall, the General Court summons Williams to answer for two incendiary letters, one he sent to the colony's churches complaining about the magistrates' treatment of him and Salem, and another addressed to his Salem church, urging the congregation to "renounce communion with all the churches in the bay, as full of antichristian pollution."

By continuing to agitate, John Cotton informs Williams, he has missed the point of his illness, has failed to learn the lesson that when God takes away one's voice one should take the hint and shut the hell up. Cotton:

> But instead of recoiling . . . you chose rather to persist in
> your way, and to protest against all the churches and
> brethren that stood in your way: and thus the good hand
> of Christ that should have humbled you, to see and turn
> from the error of your way, hath rather hardened you
> therein, and quickened you only to see failings (yea intol-

erable errors) in all the churches and brethren, rather than in yourself.

Before the court, Williams "justified both these letters, and maintained all his opinions," writes Winthrop. The court offers Williams the option of taking a few weeks to reflect and hopefully repent—"a month's respite," Winthrop calls it. I'm guessing there is no small amount of love and mercy in this offer. All the magistrates must have looked at Williams so longingly, hoping that the ride home would soften him. How could he not come around, passing through their rough-hewn New Jerusalem, going by all the humble cabins of good people who try so hard to hate themselves but love their God? How could he wave hello to the men and women with whom he sailed from England and not notice they were all in the same boat still? This cajoling had worked many times before. John Endecott, for example, had caved. He appeared before the court and "acknowledged his fault" in questioning the magistrates and Salem was granted the land in Marblehead Neck.

But Williams must have known that no amount of time, no ministerial interventions, no amount of waving hello to well-scrubbed townspeople was going to change his mind. Williams believed that a conviction, even one that is "groundless, false, and deluded . . . is not by any arguments or torments easily removed." He tells the court that he doesn't need any more time. He thinks what he thinks. Reverend Thomas Hooker is asked to debate Williams and talk him out of what Winthrop calls "his errors." Williams does not back down.

The next morning, they banish him. According to the court record, the grounds for his expulsion include spreading "new and dangerous opinions against the authority of magistrates," issuing "letters of defamation," and maintaining the aforementioned dangerous opinions "without retraction." He has six weeks to "depart out of this jurisdiction." In his journal, Winthrop adds that all the ministers (except for one, whom he fails to identify) approved the sentence.

By January, Winthrop's journal notes that, it being winter, the court had deferred Williams's expulsion until spring on the condition that he lay low and not foment unpleasantness. And yet, Winthrop writes, Williams's voice had returned and he had been preaching in his house in Salem, spewing "such points as he had been censured for." Williams "had drawn about twenty persons to his opinion . . . the people being much taken with the apprehension of his godliness." This was more than mere insubordination. There were rumors, said Winthrop, that Williams and his followers "were intended to erect a plantation about the Narragansett Bay, from whence the infection would easily spread into these churches."

Williams was no longer a member of their body—he was an infection that needed to be surgically removed. The court dispatched some men under the command of John Underhill, the Bay's militia captain, to Salem so as to drag Williams to the dock and stick him on a ship bound for England. But, writes Winthrop in his journal, "when they came at his house he had been gone three days before; but whither they could not learn."

Thirty-four years after his banishment, in a letter, Williams revealed the identity of the mole who tipped him off that the militia was coming for him to ship him back to England. Winthrop! He wrote:

> that ever-honored Governor, Mr. Winthrop, privately wrote to me to steer my course to Narragansett Bay and Indians, for many high and heavenly public ends, encouraging me, from the freeness of the place from any English claims or patents. I took his prudent motion as a hint and voice from God, and waving all other thoughts and motions, I steered my course from Salem, (though in winter snow, which I feel yet) unto these parts.

Winthrop never admits to warning Williams. As quoted above, in his journal, which he wrote with posterity in mind, Winthrop pretended to be surprised by Williams's absence and ignorant of his final destination. Obviously, if the truth came out, Winthrop's comrades on the court would have found his actions contemptible, if not downright treasonous.

This is a sappy way to put it, but the Winthrop who warns Williams is the Winthrop I fell in love with, the Winthrop Cotton Mather celebrates for sharing his firewood with the needy, the Winthrop who scolds Thomas Dudley for overcharging the poor, the Winthrop of "Christian Charity," who called for "enlargement toward others" and "brotherly affection," admonishing that "if thy brother be in want and thou canst help him . . . if thou lovest God thou must help him."

Winthrop acknowledged that if the people of Massachusetts were to stick together as members of the same body, Williams needed to be clipped off like a toenail. But Winthrop is a true Nonseparatist. Just as he refuses to give up on his old friends in the Church of England out of loyalty, affection, and respect, he must have a lingering soft spot for Williams, that "godly minister" whose arrival in Boston Winthrop recorded five years earlier. Williams apparently forgave Winthrop for being one of the magistrates who banished him; as an old man, Williams recalled fondly that Winthrop had "personally and tenderly loved me to his last breath."

In a letter he wrote in 1670, thirty-four years after his banishment, the elderly Roger Williams is clear that his icy flight from Salem that January long before was the defining event of his life, a source of strength and sorrow. "I was unkindly and unchristianly (as I believe) driven from my house and land, and wife and children (in the midst of a New England winter)," he writes.

At first, he settled down on land he purchased near present-day Rehoboth, Mass., from the Wampanoag sachem (or chief) Massasoit, remembered for the First Thanksgiving, whom Williams had befriended during his stay in Plymouth. But it turned out Massasoit was mistaken about the property line, and Williams was trespassing on Plymouth land. He soon received a letter from his old friend Edward Winslow, the Plymouth governor, "advising me (since I was fallen into their bounds, and they were loathe to displease the Bay) to remove to the other side of the water." Winslow added that once Williams vacated Plymouth's jurisdiction "we should be loving neighbors together."

Did he mention it was winter? Again from Williams's letter of 1670: "Between those my friends of the Bay and Plymouth I was sorely tossed for fourteen weeks (in a bitter winter season) not knowing what bread or bed did mean."

Apart from the humiliation of banishment and enduring—we get it!—the cold, Williams points out he suffered financial hardship since he forfeited his Salem business. He writes, "Beside the yearly loss of no small matter in my trading with English and natives, [I was] debarred from Boston (the chief mart and port of New England)." He continues, "God knows that many thousand pounds cannot repay the very temporary losses I have sustained."

His poverty must have been apparent, because when Winslow visited Williams after his family had joined him a few months later, Williams reports that Winslow "put a piece of gold into the hands of my wife for our supply."

Along with Winthrop's initial advice that Rhode Island was outside the bounds of the Massachusetts Charter, the Plymouth governor's directing him also to Rhode Island confirmed to him "the freedom and vacancy of this place, which in this respect and many other providences of the most holy and only wise, I called Providence."

Legend has it that when Williams sailed down the Seekonk River and landed at the present site of Providence, a local Narragansett greeted him, "What cheer, netop?" (a combination of the old English phrase for "How's it going?" and the Algonquian word for "friend").

The supposed site of this momentous occasion, Slate Rock, is remembered by a little monument in Providence's Slate Rock Park. Don't bother looking for the rock, though. In 2007, a Providence Parks Department official told the *Providence Journal,* "Unfortunately, in 1877, Slate Rock itself was mistakenly blown up, by city workers trying to uncover more of the rock and preserve the symbol of Williams' arrival."

Williams asked the two Narragansett sachems, the elderly Canonicus, and his younger nephew, Miantonomi, for permission to settle. Williams drew up a deed and the two men signed with their marks—a bow for Canonicus and an arrow for Miantonomi. Williams was proud of the fact that he did not buy the land. Rather it was a gift and a grant. He later boasted, "It was not price nor money that could have purchased Rhode Island. . . . Rhode Island was purchased by love."

The site of the original settlement is preserved in downtown Providence as the Roger Williams National Memorial. There, the compass and sundial Williams probably carried with him on the traumatic nature hike that got him here are on display.

Williams was soon joined by a few followers who had bolted from Massachusetts and he divided the land into equal eleven-acre plots. On August 20, 1637, these settlers signed what came to be called the Providence Agreement. It says:

> We whose names are hereunder desirous to inhabit in the town of Providence, do promise to subject ourselves in active and passive obedience, to all such orders or agreements as shall be made for public good for the body, in an orderly way, by the major consent of the present inhabitants, masters of families, incorporated together into a town fellowship, and others whom they shall admit unto them, only in civil things.

The two most important words in the agreement were, of course, "civil things." There will be no religious obedience required here.

As Williams points out in a letter to John Endecott in 1651, "My letters are not banished!" From his crude settlement, Williams keeps up an ample correspondence with his acquaintances back in Massachusetts Bay, especially John Winthrop.

Winthrop and Williams will write each other letters until Winthrop dies in 1649. Winthrop's letters to Williams have been lost, but many of Williams's many notes to Winthrop survive. They remind me a little of the letters Herman Melville sends to Nathaniel Hawthorne a couple of centuries later; Williams, like Melville, is a tad too excited, too lonely, too longwinded, too strange. At one point Melville even dreams of installing a paper mill in his house so as to provide him an endless supply of paper on which "I should write a thousand—a million—billion thoughts, all under the form of a letter to you." That sort of talk must have terrified Hawthorne. Recall Williams's apology to Winthrop for writing so many sentences "as thick and over busy as mosquitoes."

Many of Williams's letters are very hard to read. But their very difficulty might hint at why Winthrop doesn't write off his younger, weirder friend. I do not envy Glenn W. LaFantasie, editor of *The Correspondence of Roger Williams;* Williams's letters are often theologically dense, to put it mildly. One four-and-a-half-page letter to Winthrop, probably written a year or so after Williams's banishment, requires thirty-seven footnotes to explain Williams's allusions to more than thirty biblical passages. If Winthrop disagrees with many of Williams's interpretations of said passages, he cannot deny Williams's knowledge of and devotion to the Word of God.

In that letter, Williams attempts to answer a series of queries posed by Winthrop in a sort of post-banishment follow-up questionnaire. Winthrop wants to know what Williams has gained by his "newfound practices." Williams answers that he has traded in such things as "friends" and "esteem" for the "honor" of being one of Christ's witnesses, that he is "ready not only to be banished, but to die in New England for the name of the Lord Jesus." If Winthrop was hoping that a few months in exile had made Williams rethink his questionable opinions, he would have been disappointed with Williams's response, especially since Williams beseeches Winthrop to remove himself "with a holy violence from the dung heap of this earth," by which he means the Boston church. Even so, Williams is cordial toward Winthrop, addressing him as "worthy and well beloved," acknowledging that Winthrop poses his questions in the spirit of healing their rift, "as a physician to the sick."

The tone of Williams's letters and tracts addressed to John Cotton, on the other hand, is accusatory. Even Williams admits, "Some letters then passed between us, in which I proved and expressed that if I had perished in that sorrowful winter's flight, only the blood of Jesus Christ could have washed him from the guilt of mine."

Naturally, the most esteemed theologian in New England is unaccustomed to being accused of attempted manslaughter. "As if," Cotton writes Williams soon after his banishment; Williams claims to have gotten the letter in the "time of my distressed wanderings amongst the barbarians." This is the letter someone, probably Williams, published later, without Cotton's consent. In it, Cotton beseeches Williams to halt his accusations, "as if I had hastened forward the sentence of your civil banishment; for what was done by the magistrates ... was neither done by my council nor consent." Not that Cotton has a problem with the verdict: "I dare not deny the sentence passed to be righteous in the eyes of God."

Winthrop is clear in his journal that the court consulted the ministers, Cotton included. In Williams's published "Mr. Cotton's Letter Examined and Answered," Williams claimed one of the court's assistants confided in him—in tears—that the court never would have issued the verdict of banishment "had not Mr. Cotton in private given them advice." His point? Ministers in general are too influential in civil justice, and John Cotton in particular makes grown men cry.

I n 1643, seven years after his banishment, Roger Williams writes a book. He compiled *A Key into the Language of America* at sea. Williams was on his way back to England to acquire a legal charter for Providence. He worried that he would lose his Algonquian language skills abroad, skills that "I had so dearly bought in some few years of hardship and charges among the barbarians." (If the term "barbarian" seems a tad indelicate, Williams reports that the natives have an equally pejorative though more colorful name for the English: "knive-men.")

Basically, *A Key* is a souped-up dictionary arranged in chapters devoted to such subjects as sickness, fish, and the seasons of the year. There are stretches of Algonquian words and phrases arranged on the left side of the page, matched up with a column of English equivalents on the right. In between vocabulary lists, Williams makes observations about the native way of life. He ends many chapters with terrible poems in which "righteousness" rhymes with "wilderness," and "sinned" with "wind."

Though *A Key* was written long after Williams was forced out of Massachusetts to live amongst the Narragansett, it reads almost like a memoir of his banishment, giving clues about what Williams's first few months on the lam were like. Given the Algonquian words and phrases he imparts years later—such as "Sit by the fire," "Come hither, friend," and "Welcome, sleep here"—the Narragansett come off as a collective godsend. "In wilderness, in great distress," he writes, "these ravens have fed me."

Williams admits that within a two-hundred-mile radius of his home, various Algonquian-speaking tribes' "dialects do exceedingly differ, yet . . . a man may, by this help, converse with many thousands of natives all over the country." Apparently, that was still true into the twentieth century. According to Howard M. Chapin's introduction to the Rhode Island Tercentenary edition of *A Key,* published in 1936, William Brooks Cabot carried Williams's book in his knapsack as he tramped around northern Canada, wandering "the lonely wastes of Labrador with Indians who are unacquainted with the English language," and who were "Algonquians and of the same linguistic stock" as the Narragansett. In Cabot's 1912 book *In Northern Labrador,* he declares, "My objective was Indians," echoing the statement Williams made in his first surviving letter to John Winthrop way back in 1632, pining that "the Lord grant my desires . . . what I long after, the natives' souls."

Williams intends for *A Key* to help missionaries spread the gospel to American Indians, hoping "it may please the Father of Mercies to spread civility and . . . Christianity; for one candle will light ten thousand."

We will get to the Christianity spreading shortly. As for civility, Williams avows it is hardly unknown in New England's back country. "There is a savor of civility and courtesy," he says, "even amongst these wild Americans, both amongst themselves and toward strangers."

After teaching how to say "first eat something" and "bring hither some victuals," Williams writes, "If any stranger come in, they presently give him to eat of what they have." Recall that when Williams was banished he had next to nothing. He goes on, "Many a time, and at all times of the night (as I have fallen in travel upon their houses) when nothing hath been ready, have themselves and their wives, risen to prepare me some refreshing."

There is real and plain warmth in Williams's tone when he talks up Indian generosity. Relating knowledge he learned by experience, compared to the biblical minutiae he acquired by hitting the books at Cambridge, *A Key* is Williams's best writing—modest, gripping, and down to earth.

Indians make good listeners. "A deep silence they make," he writes, "and attention give to him that speaketh." Unlike some people, who throw you out of their colony just for talking.

One side effect of Williams's admiration for the natives is that they make Englishmen, including the Boston variety, look bad. That is frequently his intent. For example, in this hospitality poem, he sings,

> *I have known them leave their house and mat*
> *to lodge a friend or stranger,*
> *When Jews and Christians oft have sent*
> *Christ Jesus to the manger.*

Among his many commendations: The Narragansett enjoy a low crime rate. Natives commit "fewer scandalous sins than Europe." One "never hear[s] of robberies, rapes, murders." Also, "they never shut their doors, day nor night, and 'tis rare that any hurt is done." Plus, "Their wars are far less bloody, and devouring than the cruel wars of Europe; and seldom twenty slain in a pitch field."

Such enlargement toward others, making others' conditions their own, entertaining each other in brotherly affection—Williams's description of the Narragansett way of life sounds a lot like Winthrop's ideal of a city on a hill (just without Jehovah).

While *A Key* is the first substantive book devoted to deciphering the Algonquian language, William Wood, most likely one of the early settlers who accompanied John Endecott to Salem, had published *New England's Prospect,* a guidebook for would-be settlers, in 1634. Wood included a short glossary of Algonquian terms. Wood's descriptions of native culture generally agree with Williams's portrayal. Which is to say that Wood's interpretations of Indian society also echo Winthrop's utopian yearnings in "Christian Charity" for a caring community rejoicing and suffering together. Wood writes, "As he that kills a deer sends for his friends and eats it merrily, so he that receives but a piece of bread from an English hand parts it equally between himself and his comrades, and eats it lovingly." Wood continues, "They are love-linked thus in common courtesy."

Wood's and Williams's appreciation for the civility of New England Indians rubs off on the reader, but not as some treacly ode to noble savagery. Williams is especially interesting—and refreshing—because he regards the natives in his midst as people. In one of the goofy little poems he sprinkles throughout *A Key,* he writes, "Boast not proud English, of thy birth & blood, / thy brother Indian is by birth as good." And by "as good" he means equally deplorable, unworthy, and disgusting in the eyes of God as any of the swells in Europe: "Nature knows no difference between Europe and Americans in blood, birth, bodies, etc. God having of one blood made all mankind . . . and all by nature being children of wrath."

I can admire the inherent friendliness of native culture, just as I admire the inherent bookishness of Puritan culture, without fantasizing for one second about living in either world. I'm an indoorsy, urban woman partial to my cozy little desk job and the odd night on the town. I tend not to roman ticize traditional societies—some people just aren't cut out for that way of life. In fact, when I was forced, as a child in Oklahoma, to help out picking potatoes on what was left of my Cherokee grandfather's Indian allotment land, one day it was so humid my sweat turned the dirty field around me to mud. So I made a solemn, silent vow then and there that when I grew up I was going to buy my potatoes in a store.

In *A Key*, it's obvious, at least to me, that being a native woman in seventeenth-century New England was tough, way more difficult than being a white person or Indian man—which is saying something.

For starters, being female was literally isolating. In the chapter "Of the Family Businesses," Williams gives the words for "knife," "spoon," "wash this," and "house," along with the phrase "a woman keeping alone in her monthly sickness." The latter being a handy translation given that, in his introduction, Williams notes that during menstruation, native women are quarantined "in a little house alone by themselves four or five days, and hold it an irreligious thing for either father or husband or any male to come near them."

Indian women grind their corn by hand. Williams points out, "They plant it, dress it, gather it, barn it, beat it, and take as much pains as any people in the world, which labor is questionless one cause of their extraordinary ease of childbirth." In other words, these women's lives involved such constant, backbreaking toil and pain that delivering a baby does not faze them.

In the chapter devoted to "Eating and Entertainment," Williams points out that tobacco is the only plant tended by men, with "women managing all the rest." I.e., all nonsmokable agriculture is performed by women. In *New England's Prospect,* William Wood actually writes that while native women are "very industrious," native men "had rather starve than work." Williams doesn't entirely share Wood's dismissal of the Algonquin division of labor. Probably because Williams tags along with native men on their often harrowing hunting and fishing trips. Sounds like the former Cambridge scholar isn't exactly God's gift to the canoe. Grateful to his Narragansett lifeguards, he admits, "When sometimes in great danger I have questioned safety they have said to me: Fear not, if we be overset I will carry you safe to land."

Williams, however, is not a joiner. Considering that he is such a Separatist he won't worship with other Puritans who refuse to repent for worshipping at Anglican churches back in England, it stands to reason that he opts out of native religious ceremonies. In *A Key,* he admits that he acquired most of the facts for the chapter "Of Their Religion" by asking natives, not by observation. He tried it once and won't be doing that again: "Once being in their houses and beholding what their worship was, I durst never be an eye witness, spectator or looker on, least I should have been partaker of Satan's inventions and worships."

The man who was such a Ten Commandments stickler that he raised a stink about taking God's name in vain when Winthrop and the other magistrates administered oaths to nonbelievers, must have wanted to gouge out his own eyes looking upon what he believed to be Indians engaged in actual devil worship—a textbook violation of "You shall have no other gods before Me."

Probably one of the most useful, or at least the most telling, Algonquian phrases Williams translates in *A Key* is *Mat nowawtau hetté mina*—"We understand not each other." Also helpful: "You trouble me."

The Massachusetts Bay Colony talked a big game by putting that Indian pleading "Come over and help us" on its official seal, but few Puritans actually got around to converting Indians (much to the natives' dismay, I'm sure). Williams was the rare Englishman to take that charge seriously. But in order to talk the Narragansett into Christianity, he had to talk them out of their own religion, which he found baffling and dangerous, but nevertheless well-established and complex.

Williams notes that one of the natives' most important gods resides in the Southwest. "At the Southwest are their forefathers' souls," he writes. "To the Southwest they go themselves when they die; from the Southwest came their corn and beans."

For these beliefs, Williams concludes that "they are lost." His only hope is that a few of them "shall be found to share in the blood of the Son of God"—a very few. In a pamphlet he writes two years after *A Key,* titled *Christenings Make Not Christians,* he dismisses the idea of mass conversions of natives because he doesn't believe in mass conversion of any sort. For all his eccentricities, Williams is a conventional Calvinist regarding salvation—it's predetermined before a person is born. There is an Elect amongst Algonquian-speakers, just like there is an Elect amongst Anglophones. In the pamphlet, he points out that Jesus "abhors . . . an unwilling spouse, and to enter into a forced bed: the will in worship, if true, is like a free vote." Thus, imposing Christianity on American Indians (or anyone else) is, to Williams (and, according to Williams, Jesus) a rape of the soul. "A true conversion (whether of Americans or Europeans)," he writes, "must be by the free proclaiming or preaching of repentance and forgiveness of sins." Only then will the believer be born again, as "God's new creation in the soul."

Williams tallies up at least thirty-seven native gods—the fire god, the house god, the moon god, the sea. He even compares the natives' polytheism to the habits of "papists," who pray to such "saint protectors as St. George, St. Patrick, St. Denis, Virgin Mary, etc."

Some of the vocabulary lists in *A Key* read like transcripts of Williams's conversations:

How many gods be there?
Many, great many.

Friend, not so.

There is only one God.

You are mistaken.

Apparently, some of Christianity's more unusual articles of faith prove to be a bit of a hard sell. Williams informs one native about Christ's resurrection: "When I spoke of the rising again of the body, he cried out, 'I shall never believe this.'"

If anything, though, the New England Indians seem strangely similar to the New England Puritans. In both societies the supernatural seeps into every single facet of life on earth. Just as Massachusetts whipped up a parable of good triumphing over evil thanks to the fluke of a mouse outsmarting a snake, and John Cotton accused Roger Williams of ignoring the divine "shushhh" of his bout of laryngitis, the Narragansett also interpret their own luck as messages from their deities. One phrase in his dictionary that's equally useful in Boston or the wilderness is: "God is angry with me?"

Williams recalls one Indian man whose child had died gathering his wife and the rest of his children around him. With "an abundance of tears," the man hollered, "O God thou hast taken away my child! Thou art angry with me. O turn thine anger from me, and spare the rest of my children." On the other hand, Williams notes, "If they receive any good in hunting, fishing, harvest, etc., they acknowledge God in it."

The most intriguing Algonquian term Williams tries to

explain is *Manitou.* Manitou isn't a god per se. It's more of a supernatural force that animates certain people or things. He writes, "There is a general custom amongst them, at the apprehension of any excellency in men, women, birds, beasts, fish, etc., to cry out, 'Manitou,' that is, a god." He continues, "Thus if they see one man excel others in wisdom, valor, strength, activity, etc., they cry out, 'Manitou.'" He notes that natives are in awe of English technology. "Therefore, when they talk amongst themselves of the English ships and great buildings, of the plowings of their fields, and especially books and letters, they will end thus: *Mannittowock,* They are gods. *Cummanitoo,* You are a god."

A comedian I know, if he hears a joke that perfectly sums up some situation, comments, "You solved that." Doesn't the word *Manitou* solve the problem of accurately describing a certain kind of mysterious achievement? There's no single English word that really gets at that moment in the 1997 NBA Finals when the game was tied and Steve Kerr of the Chicago Bulls scored the winning shot with five seconds left on the clock; or this herd of elk I saw once, appearing out of the mist at twilight on a golf course in Banff; or Elliott Gould's performance in *The Long Goodbye;* or the catch in Ralph Stanley's voice when he sings "O Death."

Obviously, Williams would have his native friends exchange *Manitou* for its Judeo-Christian equivalent, divine providence. He writes of *A Key* that "this book (by God's good providence) may come into the hand of many fearing

God, who may also have many an opportunity of occasional discourse with some of these their wild brethren and sisters." And so he offers a blow-by-blow translation of how to tell the story of Creation, from the book of Genesis, in Algonquian.

He explains how to insist that "one only God . . . made all things" in six days. "The first day, He made the light," is followed by the creation of the earth and sea, the sun and the moon, the stars, birds, fish, on down to the sixth day, when "last of all He made one man of red earth and called him Adam." Then "God took a rib from Adam . . . and of that rib he made one woman."

Which is to say that Williams teaches white do-gooders how to introduce American Indians to the inheritance of original sin. Williams boasts how he ruined the peace of mind of at least one native; he recalls visiting the deathbed of a Pequot friend named Wequash. Williams had previously witnessed to Wequash about the Bible. The brokenhearted Wequash cried out in broken English, "Me so big naughty heart all one stone!"

Honestly, the idea that all human beings are corrupt vessels of evil is oppressive enough when one is born into that way of thinking. I was exposed, from infancy on, to so much wretch-like-me, original-sin talk that I spent my entire childhood believing I was as depraved as Charles Manson when in reality I might have been the best-behaved nine-year-old of the twentieth century. But how jarring it must have been to be an adult Narragansett and this strange white man shows up out of the blue and shatters his lifelong peace of mind with what the stranger calls the "good news" that the native is in fact a wicked, worthless evildoer and so was his mother. So said native dies terrified by his big, naughty, unchristian heart of stone instead of, say, as the Shawnee Tecumseh would later advise, "Sing your death song and die like a hero going home."

In *A Key*, Williams's language cushions the blow of making the acquaintance of this new deity by translating "God" as "manit," as in Manitou. But in 1663, when the Puritan John Eliot publishes his "Indian Bible," a translation of the Bible into Algonquian, God is called "God." Which is blunt. This God is different from the native gods, and Eliot does not pretend otherwise.

The irony of informing nearly naked people in a wilderness setting about the story of naked Adam and Eve eating the fruit of knowledge and inventing the fashion industry due to a sudden need for clothing to hide their shame is not lost on Williams. The natives "sleep soundly counting it a felicity," he says, quoting a proverb, "that every man be content with his skin."

One of the main points of Calvinism is to be absolutely uncomfortable and itchy and sickened in one's skin. Williams might be a little jealous when he marvels that "Adam's sons and daughters" in America "should neither have nor desire clothing for their naked souls or bodies."

The Indians' clothing-optional lifestyle affords Williams the opportunity to get in one of his jabs at European hypocrisy:

The best clad Englishman,
Not clothed in Christ, more naked is:
Than naked Indian.

Williams makes his living in Providence and its environs as he did, off and on, in Plymouth and Salem, by operating a trading post. Lucky for him, the Europeans are gaga for American fur. In the chapter called "Of Their Trading," he teaches the Algonquian word for "beaver," calling it a "beast of wonder." This part of *A Key* was surely invaluable to his readers engaged in the ever more lucrative fur trade. The reader learns how to ask, "What price?" It must have been so handy for a seventeenth-century English trapper out on the frontier of Connecticut to reach into his knapsack, pull out *A Key*, and confidently inform the Mohegan he's talking to, "I will give you an otter."

Williams seems especially amused by the fad among the European smart set for gloves and hats fashioned out of American animal pelts handled by "foul hands in smoky houses . . . which are after worn upon the hands of queens and the heads of princes."

In fact, the fur of semiaquatic North American rodents is so desirable it's literally to die for. Power struggles among the English, the Dutch, the Pequot, the Mohegan, and the Narragansett over access to and control of trade in Connecticut provokes a war.

Of all the phrases Williams translates in *A Key,* the one with the most troubling, loaded back story is this one: "The Pequots are slain."

The Pequot War is a pure war. And by pure I don't mean good. I mean it is war straight up, a war set off by murder and vengeance and fueled by misunderstanding, jealousy, hatred, stupidity, racism, lust for power, lust for land, and, most of all, greed, all of it headed toward a climax of slaughter. The English are diabolical. The Narragansett and the Mohegan are willing accomplices. The Pequot commit distasteful acts of violence and are clueless as to just how vindictive the English can be when provoked. Which is to say that there's no one to root for. Well, one could root for Pequot babies not to be burned alive, but I wouldn't get my hopes up.

As for geography, circa 1630, the Narragansett live in what would become the state of Rhode Island, hence their association with Roger Williams. The Narragansett are ruled by Canonicus and his nephew, Miantonomi. Untangling the Pequot and Mohegan is trickier as the two tribes are blood relatives with a long history of intermarriage and infighting. They control lands in Connecticut—the Mohegan on the Pequot River (now called the Thames), and the Pequot on the Connecticut River, the largest river in New England. The Mohegan have long paid tribute to the more powerful Pequot. The Mohegan sachem, Uncas, is married to the daughter of the assassinated Pequot principal sachem, Tatobem. In fact, after Tatobem's death, Uncas had thrown his hat in the ring to become Tatobem's successor but lost to Sassacus, his brother-in-law. This accounts for Uncas's animosity toward his kin the Pequot—animosity being a polite way of saying Uncas hates the Pequot's guts. Not that he has much affection for the Narragansett, either. In fact, Uncas will eventually order his brother to assassinate Miantonomi. But for now, the Mohegan and the Narragansett are allies of the English.

Why would the Mohegan and Narragansett gang up on their fellow natives the Pequot? Well, why would France, a monarchy, aid the upstart antimonarchical American colonists against its fellow monarchy England in the Revolutionary War? Simple answer: France hates England. The Pequot, the Narragansett, and the Mohegan are sovereign nations with a long history of resentment that predates European contact. And so the Mohegan and the Narragansett temporarily united in a traditional enemy-of-my-enemy-is-my-friend scenario.

After European contact, each New England tribe's power partially derives from trading with the Dutch in New Netherland and the English of Plymouth and Massachusetts Bay.

Uncas, a brilliant, forward-thinking opportunist, gambles his small, relatively powerless tribe's fortunes and throws in with the English. Boy does this pay off. For this reason, Uncas is probably the most controversial historical figure in seventeenth-century New England. His brutality toward his brother Pequot comes off as morally sickening. And yet his tiny, dwindling tribe, under the Pequot thumb and decimated by the smallpox epidemic of 1633, is on the verge of extinction. As sachem, his responsibility is to save his people any way he knows how, and becoming an English ally is the most logical course of action. If the sachem's name is ringing a bell, that's because James Fenimore Cooper snagged it as the name of a character in *The Last of the Mohicans,* his novel romanticizing the natives' disappearing way of life. Real-life Uncas is taking drastic steps to stave off such oblivion, and he more or less succeeds.

By the time the Winthrop fleet arrived in Massachusetts in 1630, the Dutch of New Netherland had already ushered in what Neal Salisbury, author of *Manitou and Providence,* calls "the wampum revolution." Wampum, strings of white and purple beads made out of clam and conch shells found primarily on Long Island but also in Narragansett Bay, was a form of Indian currency that had originally been more of a sacred object than mere money.

Salisbury writes that "the critical point in the rise of the Narragansett and the Pequot" came about in 1622, when a Dutch trader kidnapped a Pequot sachem "and threatened to behead him if he did not receive 'a heavy ransom.'" The Dutchman received 140 strings of wampum right away and, "as a result . . . the Dutch West India Company discovered both the value to the Indians of wampum and the power and prestige of the Pequot." Furthermore, Salisbury says, the resulting wampum craze "reinforced the dominant position of the Narragansett and particularly the Pequot, both of whom already had access to the prized shells." (The two tribes' power is also a testament to strength in numbers, both groups lucking out and being spared by the smallpox epidemic of 1619 that exterminated so many Indians in Massachusetts, though the epidemic of 1633 would affect them severely.)

The coastal Indians' wampum could be traded for animal pelts trapped by Indians living in the continent's interior, which would in turn be exported to Europe. The perfect symbol of this exchange is depicted in the official seal of New Netherland, which depicts a beaver surrounded by a string of wampum.

Put the rather frank Dutch seal next to Massachusetts Bay's overly optimistic seal with that Indian pleading, "Come Over and Help Us"—and it's easy to figure out the main concerns of white settlers in the Northeast: trade, God, and "fixing" the Indians.

On October 2, 1633, Winthrop writes in his journal about the return of his personal trading boat, *The Blessing of the Bay,* which he had sent south to Long Island and New Amsterdam. In the latter city, the Massachusetts men presented the Dutch governor with a letter explaining that Connecticut belonged to the king of England. They returned home with a "very courteous and respectful" letter for Winthrop in which the Dutchman countered that he believed Connecticut belonged to the Dutch West India Company but perhaps the company and the king should work it out themselves back in Europe.

That's a reminder just how new European settlement in the New World still is. In 1633, Connecticut is the frontier.

In the same entry, Winthrop reports that even though the Dutch had already erected a trading post on the Connecticut River—on the site of present-day Hartford—Plymouth built its own spiteful post a mile upriver of the Dutch, thus cutting off much of the Dutch supply of furs. Such territorial spats did not sour Winthrop on Connecticut, though. He reports, erroneously, that the river runs so far north it "comes within a day's journey of . . . the 'Great Lake,'" presumably Lake Champlain. His lust for it is palpable when he writes, "From this lake, and the hideous swamps about it, come most of the beaver which is traded between Virginia and Canada." Needless to say, that's a lot of beaver.

The Dutch in Connecticut, meanwhile, have been trading with the Pequot, but with other Indians, too. How do the Pequot feel about this? They murder a handful of Indians, probably Narragansett, on their way home from trading with the Dutch.

To show the Pequot who's boss, the Dutch kidnap Tatobem, the principal sachem of the Pequot, and demand a
ransom of wampum for his return. After receiving the wam
pum, the Dutch do send Tatobem back to the Pequot—his
dead body.

Start keeping score.

Surprise, surprise, the Pequot retaliate. Which makes a
certain amount of eye-for-an-eye sense. Except that in the
dumbest of all possible moves, the Pequot take revenge on
the Dutch by killing a white boat captain on the Connecticut
River who turns out to be an Englishman. They all look alike,
right?

On the bright side, the Pequot have murdered Captain
John Stone, a pirate of such loose morals he has been banished from Massachusetts Bay. And not for high-minded,
theological differences of opinion, either. According to Winthrop's journal, Stone got the boot in 1633 because he was
found "in the drink" and in bed "with one Bancroft's wife."
Stone was tried before the court and fined one hundred
pounds—quite a sum in seventeenth-century Boston—and
"ordered upon pain of death to come here no more."

If a Pequot were going to murder a colonist from Massachusetts, picking one who faced the death sentence if he
ever set foot in Massachusetts again would be a lucky one to
kill. And at first, that's true. When he hears about Stone's
death, Winthrop says in his journal that he plans to write the
governor of Virginia about a reprisal since "Stone was of that

colony." Stone was no longer "of" Massachusetts, so he's someone else's problem. That's in January of 1634. By November, however, the English demand that the Pequot turn over Stone's murderers. Winthrop doesn't explain the gradual change of heart but my guess is that a turf war over Connecticut becomes increasingly inevitable and the English are ready to pick a fight.

The buildup to the Pequot War reminds me of what skateboarders call the frustration that makes them occasionally break their own skateboards in half—"focusing your board." The Pequot War is just that—a destructive tantrum brought on by an accumulation of aggravation.

In September 1634, the esteemed minister of the church at New Town, Thomas Hooker (the Puritan dissident who sailed on the same boat as John Cotton), petitions the General Court on behalf of his congregation. Hooker informs the court that they want to leave the Boston area and settle in Connecticut. One of their reasons for going, according to Winthrop's journal, is "the fruitfulness and commodiousness of Connecticut, and the danger of having it possessed by others, Dutch or English." (And by English they mean the Plymouth folk.) Of course, Winthrop, who really does believe the things he said in "Christian Charity" about how the colonists should be knit together as members of the same body, is loathe to lose any of the godly. He is especially despondent about Hooker's possible defection, writing that the minister's exit would be a great loss as "the removing of a candlestick is a great judgment, which is to be avoided." The candlestick, in Puritan lingo, is one of Christ's lights, an important, beloved object of admiration that draws in other worshippers as moths to flame. Winthrop fails to notice that Hooker is in the same position Winthrop himself was in leaving England—being accused of abandoning his countrymen in their time of need. Remember, Winthrop had helped write that pro-emigration tract back in England that claimed "The departing of good people from a country does not cause a judgment, but warns of it."

The murder of Stone in Connecticut and the threat of losing Hooker's congregation to Connecticut is happening right around the time that Salem cuts the king's cross out of the flag, Roger Williams is still in his prebanishment, mouthing-off period, and Bishop Laud demands the Charter be sent back to England. Winthrop is hardly paranoid to worry that the colony is on the verge of falling apart.

The magistrates temporarily talk Hooker and his flock into tabling their move, especially since it "would expose them to evident peril, both from the Dutch . . . and from the Indians." But within two years, Hooker would lead his people to Connecticut to found Hartford, just in time for the full-blown Pequot War.

In November 1634, the Pequot send two ambassadors to Boston to meet with Winthrop and the other assistants, who tell the pair that Boston's friendship is conditional upon the Pequot turning over the murderers of Captain Stone. They reply that all but two of the perpetrators have since died of smallpox. (A devastating epidemic has recently wreaked havoc amongst the Pequot, Mohegan, and Narragansett.) Winthrop notes of the Pequot testimony, "This was related with such confidence and gravity, as, having no means to contradict it, we inclined to believe it."

So far so good. Winthrop also notes that the Pequot were desperate for allies: "The reason why they desired so much our friendship was because they were now in war with the Narragansett." As a result, "they could not trade safely anywhere."

The Pequot representatives agree to a treaty. Per Winthrop, they are to "deliver us the two men who were guilty of Capt. Stone's death," as well as "give us four hundred fathom of wampum, and forty beaver, and thirty otter skins." Oh, and also: "to yield up Connecticut." If that sounds like a lot, it's because it is. But Winthrop says the Pequot request that the English "settle a plantation there." They want the English there to trade with them, and for protection.

The next morning, Winthrop says, some Narragansett are rumored to be lurking nearby in order to ambush the Pequot ambassadors. The English talk the Narragansett into leaving, promising them that if they make peace with the Pequot, the English will give them a portion of the tribute wampum.

The following year, that being 1635, Winthrop reports that on the same ship Henry Vane sailed in on, his son, John

Winthrop, Jr., returns from a trip abroad with a commission in hand from a group of English nobles to "begin a plantation at Connecticut and be governor there." The settlement and its strategically important fort, where the Connecticut River meets Long Island Sound, will be named Saybrook, in honor of two of the nobles: Viscount Say and Sele, and Lord Brook.

Then, in May of 1636, Winthrop writes that the twenty-four-year-old Henry Vane is elected to be governor of the Massachusetts Bay Colony and "Mr. Hooker . . . and most of his congregation went to Connecticut." Though his journal is of course mum, Winthrop must be worried about the state of things—a youngster is running the colony, there's this Connecticut brain drain to worry about, and he's still reeling from Roger Williams's banishment in January.

But it turns out that banishing Roger Williams was the smartest thing the Massachusetts Bay Colony ever did, in terms of cinching its status as *the* New England superpower. And not just because his rebellious opinions were undermining the Bay's monolithic conformity. As Williams would so bluntly describe his own history with New England Indians, "God was pleased to give me a painful, patient spirit to lodge with them in their filthy, smoky holes (even while I lived at Plymouth and Salem) to gain their tongue." So he was already proficient in the Algonquian language and well known as a friend to natives by the time the Narragansett took him in. Within a year of Massachusetts kicking him out,

Massachusetts was using Williams as its Indian ambassador, negotiator, and spy.

Oddly enough, he was happy to help. "I am not yet turned Indian," Williams writes Winthrop. But he had turned Indian enough to meddle on Boston's behalf.

In a letter Williams wrote later (1670), he recalled, "When the next year after my banishment, the Lord drew the bow of the Pequot War against the [English] . . . I had my share of service to the whole land in that Pequot business, inferior to very few that acted."

Williams goes on to say that after receiving letters from the Boston government requesting that he "use my utmost and speediest endeavors to break and hinder the league labored for by the Pequots against . . . the English," he set off toward Pequot headquarters in his canoe in a storm. Once he got there, he for several days was forced "to lodge and mix with the bloody Pequot ambassadors, whose hands and arms (me thought) wreaked with the blood of my countrymen murdered and massacred by them on the Connecticut River." He was so scared of them, "I could not but nightly look for their bloody knives at my own throat also."

Williams's geographical location in Providence situated him much closer to the Connecticut River Valley than far-away Boston. That, coupled with his language skills and Indian alliances, made him a crucial participant. In that same 1670 letter, he claims he was so helpful that John Winthrop lobbied to have his banishment rescinded. Williams writes that Winthrop "and some of other council motioned, and it was debated, whether or no I had merited not only to be recalled from banishment, but also to be honored with some remark of favor." Of course the banishment remained in place. Williams writes cryptically that he was thwarted by one "who never favored the liberty of other men's consciences." In other words, he blames John Cotton.

Winthrop's journal entry for July 20, 1636, remarks that a trader named John Gallop who was on his way to Long Island was forced by a windstorm to put in at Block Island (currently part of the state of Rhode Island). Gallop spotted a boat he recognized as belonging to his fellow Bay Colony resident John Oldham, "a member of the Watertown congregation." Gallop shouted hello to Oldham "but had no answer." Plus, the deck of Oldham's boat was "full of Indians (fourteen in all)." Gallop suspected foul play, as the Indians were "armed with guns, pikes, and swords." Gallop steered his boat to bash into Oldham's and scared the Indians. Ten of them jumped into the water and drowned. Gallop and the two boys who were with him came aboard Oldham's boat, tied up two Indians on deck, but, "being well acquainted with their skill to untie themselves . . . he threw them bound into the sea."

They found Oldham's body under an old fishing net, "stark naked, his head cleft to the brains, and his hand and legs cut as if [the Indians] had been cutting them off, and yet warm."

The Bay Colony had slowly worked themselves up into a rage for retribution over the murder of Captain Stone, a drunken adulterer they themselves would have killed if he was ever daft enough to return to Massachusetts. Oldham, on the other hand, was one of them, a church member, a member of the same body. That Indians had bashed in his brains and attempted to dismember him was in and of itself reason enough to mow down his murderers. That the killing happened after two years of Massachusetts's jitters about Indian behavior south of its border meant war.

Two natives who understood the colonists' state of mind, and wisely tripped all over themselves to remain on the Bay Colony's good side, were Canonicus and Miantonomi, the Narragansett sachems. The following week, Canonicus sent three messengers, two of whom were eyewitnesses to Oldham's murder, to Boston. They brought a letter from Roger Williams and news that Miantonomi was already "gone with seventeen canoes and two hundred men to take revenge."

Winthrop says Massachusetts authorities interrogated one of the three Narragansett messengers. He divulged that Oldham's murderers were Niantic allies of the Narragansett who, unbeknownst to Canonicus and Miantonomi, killed Oldham because he traded with the Pequot.

Winthrop records that Governor Vane wrote to Roger Williams to watch his back "if we should have occasion to make war upon the Narragansett, for Block Island was under them."

In other words, at this point, war with the Pequot is still not a foregone conclusion. But the Pequot's chief rivals, the Narragansett, with help from Roger Williams, have acted quickly and shrewdly to win over the Bay Colony to their side.

Boston soon receives word from Miantonomi, that he is on the Niantic case and that he has a hundred fathom of Oldham's wampum to send to Boston. (By contrast, Boston is still waiting to receive the reparation wampum they had demanded from the Pequot more than a year earlier.) The following week, Boston sends representatives to Miantono- mi's co-sachem, Canonicus, to shore up its alliance with the Narragansett. Winthrop writes with relief that the sachem has "great command over his men, and marvelous wisdom in his answers and the carriage of the whole treaty, clearing himself and his neighbors of the murder, and offering assis- tance for revenge of it."

On August 25, 1636, Winthrop records in his journal that Governor Vane, along with the magistrates and ministers meet "about doing justice upon the Indians for the death of Mr. Oldham" and agree to deputize a posse posthaste. They dispatch ninety men divided amongst four captains, includ- ing John Underhill, under the general command of Salem's John Endecott.

Boston is cleaning house. The expedition's mission is twofold. Winthrop writes, "They had commission to put to death the men of Block Island, but to spare the women and children . . . and from thence go to the Pequot to demand the murderers of Captain Stone," along with one thousand fathom of wampum. If they are refused the perpetrators and the booty, the men are to kidnap Pequot children as ransom. Snatching kids away from their mothers as a military plan would be horrifying except for the fact that—spoiler alert— what the English end up doing to the Pequot youngsters is way, way worse than kidnapping.

As if there isn't enough to worry about, the devil's sorcerers are plotting against them. Roger Williams sends a disquieting letter, informing Boston that "The Pequots hear of your preparations . . . and comfort themselves in this that a witch amongst them will sink" the English boats "by diving under water and making holes." Williams adds, "I hope their dreams through the mercy of the Lord shall vanish, and the devil and his lying sorcerers shall be confounded."

Do keep in mind Williams's warning of underwater witches as we witness the ugliness ahead. To modern readers, the Pequot War is an unpleasant turf war in which the English battle a specific New England tribe. To the English, they are fighting the devil himself and his earthly representatives.

John Endecott, John Underhill, and their men sail to Block Island. Underhill would go on to write a gripping memoir of the Pequot War, titled *News from America.* In it, he says that when they pull up along the island's shore, around fifty natives are lying in wait. They let loose their arrows, Underhill writes, "as though they had meant to have made an end of us all in a moment." One Englishman is hit in the neck, but because he is wearing a collar so stiff "as if it had been an oaken board," his life is spared. Similarly, Underhill relates that had his wife not nagged him into wearing his helmet, he would have been "slain" by an arrow through the forehead. "The arrows flying thick about us, we made haste to the shore," he writes. Luckily, he points out, "Our bullets out-reach their arrows."

They make camp. The next day, they set off to kill the islanders, but the islanders have hidden in the swamps. Since the English can't find anyone to shoot at, they spend the day "burning and spoiling the land." The following day, more of same. The English "burnt their houses" and "cut down their corn." Still, no Indians to be found. So Underhill admits the following distasteful fact: the English, denied the human targets they came for, "destroyed some of their dogs instead of men."

The Block Islanders never come out. So the demoralized English slink off toward Connecticut to confront the Pequot. Once they get there, Underhill writes, some Pequot on shore spot their boats and call out, "What cheer, Englishmen? What do you come for?" The English do not answer them. The Indians nevertheless follow them. Underhill says the Pequot run along the bank of the Pequot River (now the Thames), asking, "Are you hoggery? Will you cram us? That is, are you angry, will you kill us, do you come to fight?"

That evening, Underhill says, the English remain on the

river, in their boats. The Niantic and Pequot build fires on either riverbank so the English won't "land in the night." Underhill complains that, "they made the most doleful and woeful cries all the night (so that we could scarce rest)."

The next day, according to Underhill the English are approached by a Pequot, "a grave senior, a man of good understanding, portly, carriage grave, and majestical in his expressions. He demanded of us what the end of our coming was."

They answer that the government of the Bay has sent them to bring back the heads of the men who murdered Captain Stone. "It was not the custom of the English to suffer murderers to live," they explain. "Therefore, if the Pequot desired their own peace and welfare, they will peaceably answer our expectation and give us the heads of the murderers."

"They being a witty and ingenious nation," Underhill remarks, the old man insisted they knew "not that any of ours have slain any English." Then he told them about a trading boat that came up their river and how the men on it lured their sachem on board and then informed the tribe that if they wanted him back to give them a bushel of wampum. "This peal did ring terribly in our ears," the old man explained. So, he said, the Pequot gave the kidnappers what they asked and the kidnappers returned the sachem to shore, "but first slew him." Seeing the corpse of their leader, he said, "made us vow a revenge."

The elder ambassador continues. When another white man's boat showed up, that being Captain Stone's, the dead sachem's son went aboard. "Stone, having drunk more than did him good, fell backwards on the bed asleep." So the sachem's son took out his hatchet and "therewith knocked him in the head." The old man asks, "Could ye blame us for revenging so cruel a murder? For we distinguish not between the Dutch and the English, but took them to be one nation. And therefore, we do not conceive that we wronged you."

The English aren't buying it. They tell the ambassador that his people have had more than enough contact with the English and the Dutch to tell the two apart. "Seeing you have slain the king of England's subjects, we came to demand an account of their blood."

The old man then counters, essentially, No, really, we can't tell you people apart. Then the English tell him that can't be true. "We must have the heads of those persons that have slain ours or we will fight you."

The old man asks them to wait in their boat and he will go to his people and bring back an answer. When the soldiers follow him ashore, he insists the Englishmen wait in a spot they quickly determine is the most vulnerable position around. "They carried themselves very subtly," Underhill remarks of the old man's smarts. He comes back and says the sachem has gone to Long Island.

The English tell him they don't believe this and if the Pequot don't produce the sachem forthwith, the soldiers will "beat up the drum and march through the country and spoil your corn."

So the old man tells the English to wait. So they do. Then they wait some more. Then they notice, while they're waiting, that the Pequot are leading away their women and children and burying things of value. In other words, preparing either for battle or escape. When a messenger tells the English the sachem will see them if they will lay down their arms, the English say no and the Pequot laugh at them for waiting so long, so the English start shooting willy-nilly and the Pequot run off and the English dig up the Pequot's stuff and take it, says Underhill, as booty. Then, just as they had done on Block Island, Underhill writes, "We spent the day burning and spoiling the country." And, "having burnt and spoiled what we could light on, we embarked our men and set sail for the Bay."

Winthrop's journal records with delight that the men "came all safe to Boston, which was a marvelous providence of God, that not a hair fell from the head of any of them." Not only that, but on their way home, they were accompanied by a Narragansett interpreter who killed a Pequot in a swamp along the way and "flayed off the skin of his head," i.e., scalped him. So: bonus.

The jubilation, however, is short-lived when Winthrop hears from Williams that the Pequot are attempting not only to make peace with the Narragansett but "had labored to persuade them that the English were minded to destroy all Indians." Boston is alarmed enough by the possibility of a Pequot-Narragansett alliance, according to Winthrop, that they send for Miantonomi right away.

By the time Miantonomi arrives in Boston, there have been more skirmishes between the Pequot and the settlers in Saybrook.

According to Winthrop's journal entry for October 21, 1636, Miantonomi addresses an assembly of Boston's magistrates and ministers. He reassures them "That [the Narragansett] had always loved the English, and desired firm peace with us" and "that they would continue in war with the Pequot and their confederates."

Boston draws up a formal agreement with Miantonomi, but since he doesn't entirely understand the articles of the treaty, Winthrop says, "We agreed to send a copy of them to Mr. Williams who could best interpret them to them." The treaty calls for "neither party to make peace with the Pequot without the other's consent"; "not to harbor the Pequots"; "to put to death or deliver over murderers"; and "free trade between us."

If only every English ally were as cordial as Miantonomi. In the same entry, Winthrop reports receiving a snippy letter from Governor Bradford in Plymouth complaining that Boston had "occasioned a war by provoking the Pequot," thus placing Plymouth in harm's way. Winthrop admits the letter irks him. "The deputy took it ill" is how he puts it. He writes back to Bradford, "We went not to make war upon them, but to do justice."

In this same action-packed journal entry about the treaty with the Narragansett and the displeasure of Plymouth, Winthrop brings up "one Mrs. Hutchinson, a member of the church of Boston" and her "dangerous errors." This is the first time Winthrop mentions Anne Hutchinson. The years 1636–37 are busy and difficult: Boston banishes Roger Williams, prepares to go to war against the king of England, does go to war with the Pequot, watches Connecticut draw away some of its best citizens, and deals with Anne Hutchinson, a female blabbermouth who is so difficult and so defiant that the General Court will long for the good old days of bickering with the comparatively easygoing Williams.

By January of 1637, Winthrop's journal notes that "a general fast was kept in all the churches." The Massachusetts Bay colonists diet en masse to appease God for an accumulation of sins and worries—everything from the "bishops making havoc" back home with their "popish ceremonies and doctrines" to "the dangers of those at Connecticut, and of ourselves also, by the Indians," as well as "the dissensions in our churches," by which he means the recent Hutchinson hubbub.

By March, good old Miantonomi sends Boston a tribute of "forty fathom of wampum and a Pequot's hand," severed body parts being the seventeenth-century equivalent of a gift basket of mini-muffins. Also, the Connecticut settlers send word that they are, per Winthrop's Journal, "unsatisfied with our former expedition of the Pequot, and their expectations of a further prosecution of the war." To that end, Boston dispatches Captain John Underhill to Saybrook.

May of 1637 is the most eventful month in an eventful year. Partly as a result of his firm hand (which is to say hypercritical severity—a Puritan selling point) throughout the Anne Hutchinson crisis, Winthrop is reelected governor for the first time in three years. There's news from Connecticut that the Pequot killed nine English settlers and kidnapped two English girls. And Roger Williams, acting as the Bay Colony's go-between with the Narragansett, sends a letter to Boston reporting that "our neighbor princes," i.e., Canonicus and Miantonomi, have been made aware of "your intentions and preparations against the common enemy, the Pequot."

"Miantonomi kept his barbarous court lately at my house," Williams continues. Then he boasts, "He takes some pleasure to visit me." The Narragansett send along a list of suggestions and requests for joining the English in combat, including advising the English to attack the Pequot at night "when they are commonly more secure at home, by which advantage [they] may enter the houses and do what execution they please."

For their trouble, Williams writes that Canonicus would "gladly accept a box of eight or ten pounds of sugar." He also notes "that it would be pleasing to all natives, that women and children be spared." At the end of Williams's letter is a helpful map of the Connecticut River area, including where the Pequot forts are, including the location of the principal sachem, Sassacus.

Captain John Mason, a former Bostonian who had settled in Connecticut, leads a force of colonists and Mohegan allies under the command of Uncas to Fort Saybrook, where they will meet up with the Boston soldiers under the command of John Underhill and the Narragansett. Mason and Uncas split up, with Mason's forces going by boat and Uncas's men going on foot. Mason was dubious at best whether he could count on Uncas. He would soon find out that the English could always count on Uncas.

Not only did Uncas show up at the fort, as promised, he and his men got into a scrape with some Pequot on the way there and brought back five severed Pequot heads to prove it. Mason, who, like Underhill, wrote a memoir of the conflict—*A Brief History of the Pequot War*—enthuses that the English saw the decapitations as "a special providence; for before we were somewhat doubtful of [Uncas's] fidelity." Underhill uses the same word to describe the Mohegan commitment in *News from America:* "This mightily encouraged the hearts of all, and we took this as a pledge of their further fidelity."

More good news. Oh, but what could be better news than a bouquet of enemy heads rolling around the fort's floor? Live English girls. Underhill relates that brave Dutch traders dispatched by the governor of New Netherland rescued the two Connecticut maids who had been kidnapped by the Pequot and return them to the fort. The eldest girl, who is sixteen, especially impresses the men. Underhill writes, "She told us [the Pequot] did solicit her to uncleanness, but her heart being much broken," she asked them, "How shall I commit this great evil and sin against my God?" Fearing "God's displeasure with them," the Pequot didn't touch either girl. Still, Underhill recounts, "hope was their chiefest food and tears their constant drink." The girl recalls that she lost hope and worried her captors would kill her, especially if the war came.

Then she had a most Calvinist epiphany. She asked herself, "Why should I distrust God? Do I not daily see the love of God to my poor, distressed soul? And he hath said that he will never leave me, nor forsake me." Realizing this, she resolved, "I will not fear what man can do unto me, knowing God to be above man, and man can do nothing without God's permission."

Underhill is clearly awed by the girl's pious pluck. She inspires him to think of celebrated would-be martyrs of the Old Testament, like Shadrach, Meshach, and Abednego, like Daniel in the lion's den: "Better in a fiery furnace with the presence of Christ, than in a kingly palace without him. Better in the lion's den, in the midst of all the roaring lions with Christ, than in a down bed with wife and children without Christ."

Thus are the English troops spiritually nurtured by the released Calvinist captive, and in good spirits due to Uncas's so very thoughtful decapitation offering, when Miantonomi and his army arrive to help out. Mason recalls that the Narragansett gathered themselves "into a ring, one by one, making solemn protestations how gallantly they would [carry] themselves and how many men they would kill."

Mason reports that on May 25, "about eight of the clock in the morning, we marched thence toward the Pequot, with about five hundred Indians." Their original aim was to attack the headquarters of Sassacus, the Pequot sachem. After all, it was Sassacus who had murdered Captain Stone to avenge his father's death. But at some point, they decide to attack the Pequot fort at Mystic instead. It's closer.

As the day wears on, they get hotter and hungrier, and Mason says that "some of our men fainted."

"I then inquired of Uncas," he writes, asking "what he thought the Indians would do?" Uncas predicts, "The Narragansetts would all leave us." As for the Mohegan, Uncas reassures Mason that "he would never leave us: and so it proved: For which expressions and some other speeches of his, I shall never forget him. Indeed he was a great friend, and did great service."

At night, recalls Mason, "the rocks were our pillows; yet rest was pleasant."

The next morning, Mason asks Uncas and his comrade, Wequash—the same Wequash whose deathbed lamentations Roger Williams recounts in A Key—where the fort is. They tell him it's on top of a nearby hill. Looking around,

Mason wonders where the hell the Narragansett have disappeared to. They are nowhere to be seen. Uncas replies that they're hanging back, "exceedingly afraid." Mason tells Uncas and Wequash not to leave but to stand back and wait to see "whether Englishmen would now fight or not."

Then Underhill joins in the huddle and he and Mason begin "commending ourselves to God." They divide their men in half, "there being two entrances to the fort."

The Pequot fort is encircled within a palisade—a wall made of thick tree trunks standing up and fastened together. Around seven hundred men, women, and children are asleep in wigwams inside.

Mason writes that they "heard a dog bark." Their sneak attack is foiled. The Pequot Paul Revere alerts the town. Mason says they heard "an Indian crying *Owanux! Owanux!* Which is Englishmen! Englishmen!"

Mason: "We called up our forces with all expedition, gave fire upon them through the palisade, the Indians being in a dead—indeed their last—sleep."

Mason commands the Narragansett and Mohegan to surround the palisade in what Underhill describes as a "ring battalia, giving a volley of shot upon the fort." Hearing gunfire, the awakened Pequot, writes Underhill, "brake forth into the most doleful cry."

The Pequot screams are so doleful Underhill says the English almost sympathize with their prey—almost. Until the English manage to remember why they are there in the first place (to avenge the murder of various Englishmen, from a drunken, wife-stealing pirate to the settlers on the Connecticut frontier when those girls were kidnapped). Thus Underhill reports, "Every man being bereaved of pity fell upon the work without compassion, considering the blood [the Pequot] had shed of our native countrymen."

Then the English enter the fort, carrying, per Underhill, "our swords in our right hand, our carbines or muskets in our left hand." Mason and Underhill start knocking heads inside the wigwams. Various Pequot come at them. "Most courageously these Pequot behaved themselves," Underhill will praise them later on.

Combat in the cozy little bark houses is chaos—too dangerous and unpredictable. Mason is hit with arrows and Underhill's hip is grazed. Mason is faced, on a smaller scale, with the same problem Harry Truman would confront when he was forced to ponder the logistics of invading Japan in 1945. A ground war would damn untold thousands of American troops to certain slaughter. The Puritan commander, in a smaller, grubbier, lower-tech way, arrives at the same conclusion as Truman when he ordered the bombing of Hiroshima and Nagasaki. Mason says, "We must burn them."

And they do.

Mason dashes inside a hut, lights a torch, and "set the wigwam on fire." The inhabitants are stunned. "When it was thoroughly kindled," Mason recalls, "the Indians ran as men most dreadfully amazed."

Underhill, too, lights up his vicinity, and "the fires of both meeting in the center of the fort blazed most terribly and burnt all in the space of half an hour."

The wind helps. According to Mason, the fire "did swiftly overrun the fort, to the extreme amazement of the enemy, and great rejoicing of ourselves." Mason notes that some of the Indians try to climb over the palisade and others start "running into the very flames." They shoot arrows at the Englishmen, who answer them with gunfire, but, writes Underhill, "the fire burnt their very bowstrings."

"Mercy they did deserve for their valor," Underhill admits of the Pequot. Not that they get any. William Bradford was told by a participant that "it was a fearful sight to see them thus frying in the fire, and the streams of blood quenching the same, and horrible was the stink and scent thereof."

The Englishmen escape the flames and then guard the two exits so that no Pequot can escape. According to Underhill, those who try to get away "our soldiers entertained with the point of the sword; down fell men, women, and children."

Mason summarizes, "And thus . . . in little more than an hour's space was their impregnable fort with themselves utterly destroyed, to the number of six or seven hundred." That's right—as many as seven hundred people, some of them babies, some of them those babies' mothers, were burned alive in their homes.

Two Englishmen die and about twenty are wounded.

Mason is triumphant. After all, this is the will of a righteous God. He praises the Lord for "burning them up in the fire of his wrath, and dunging the ground with their flesh: It is the Lord's doings, and it is marvelous in our eyes!" That might be the creepiest exclamation point in American literature. No, wait—it's this one: "Thus did the Lord judge among the heathen, filling the place with dead bodies!"

Underhill has read enough of the New Testament to at least pretend to stop and question this human barbecue. He asks, "Should not Christians have more mercy and compassion?" Answer: Nope. The Bible offers reasoning enough: "When a people is grown to such a height of blood and sin against God and man . . . there He hath no respect to persons, but harrows them and saws them and puts them to the sword and the most terriblest death that may be." Even children? Yes. "Sometimes," Underhill continues, "the scripture declareth women and children must perish with their parents." He concludes, "We had sufficient light from the word of God for our proceedings."

For Underhill, biblical justification is enough of an air freshener to erase the smell of burning human flesh. But the Narragansett and Mohegan, whom Underhill calls "our Indians," were shaken by the viciousness of the English and the horror of the carnage. Especially the Narragansett. Recall they had explicitly asked before the campaign, via Roger Williams, "that it would be pleasing to all natives, that women and children be spared."

"Our Indians," Underhill writes, "came to us and much

rejoiced at our victories, and greatly admired the manner of Englishmen's fight, but cried *'Much it, much it,'* that is, 'It is naught, it is naught, because it is too furious and slays too many men.'" The word "naught," to a seventeenth-century English speaker, meant "evil."

In 1889, a statue of Mason drawing his sword was erected on the site of the Mystic Fort massacre, in the present-day town of Groton. In 1992, a Pequot named Wolf Jackson petitioned the town council to remove the statue. According to the *Hartford Courant,* in one of the meetings in which the statue's fate was debated, one citizen proclaimed "that the statue on Pequot Avenue is about as appropriate as a monument at Auschwitz to Heinrich Himmler, architect of the Nazis' Final Solution." As a compromise between the faction who wanted the statue destroyed and boosters who wanted to keep it in place, in 1996 the statue was moved away from the site of the massacre to nearby Windsor, which was founded by Mason. The *New York Times* reported that nine protestors attended the rededication ceremony: "'No Hero,' said one sign; 'Remember the Pequot Massacres,' said another." A few weeks later, vandals doused the bronze Mason with red paint.

After the Mystic Fort Massacre, there are a few more dwindling skirmishes here and there in the Pequot War. Individual Pequot are hunted down by other Indians, who decapitate their corpses and send their severed heads along to the English, including the head of the principal sachem, Sassacus, who is beheaded by Mohawks. These grisly trophies, reports Mason, "came almost daily to Windsor or Hartford." But Mystic more or less marks the end of the Pequot War, as well as the end of Pequot power.

Captured Pequot are divvied up as spoils among the victors. Boston sells some of its share of Pequot survivors into slavery in Bermuda. (Many Pequot descendants still live on Bermuda's St. David's Island, their Indian slave ancestors having intermarried with their African slave ancestors.) In 1638, the Connecticut English host a treaty party in Hartford where a few remaining Pequot are divided among Uncas, Miantonomi, and the leaders of other tribes that had been English allies. The treaty mandates that the Pequot are to be absorbed into their adoptive tribes, their own tribal identity outlawed. "The Pequots were then bound by covenant," writes Mason, "that none should inhabit their native country, nor should any of them be called Pequots any more, but Mohegans and Narragansetts forever." After trying to physically annihilate the Pequot, the English attempt to wipe out the Pequot linguistically, forbidding the tribe to refer to themselves as Pequot.

The Pequot absorbed into Uncas's tribe later became known as the Mashantucket Pequot. In 1976, this tribe successfully sued the state of Connecticut for recovery of some of its land in Connecticut and received federal recognition from Ronald Reagan in 1983. This is the home to the tribe's wildly profitable Foxwoods Resort Casino.

O n our Plymouth-bound vacation, my sister Amy, my
nephew Owen, and I visit the Mashantucket Pequot
Museum, a stone's throw from Foxwoods. It's an impressive
facility with a tower where visitors can look across the tree-
tops and admire the landscape and the casino's teal roof. The
museum features life-size dioramas with mannequins de-
picting the Pequot way of life, including a caribou hunt and a
wigwam village enclosed in a palisade like the one at Mystic.
Inside, a child naps on a bed of animal skins, a woman guts a
fish, an elder teaches a teenager how to make an arrow.

We sit in the museum's theater and watch a film— a dramatic reenactment of the massacre at the Mystic fort. Owen is
seven. His knowledge of seventeenth-century New England
derives entirely from what he learned in his school's Thanksgiving pageant the previous fall and repeated viewings of
Scooby-Doo and the Witch's Ghost, in which a cartoon dog and
his teenage friends visit a haunted New England town.

When the film shows the Pequot clashing with Connecticut settlers, Owen whispers, "I don't get it. Why are they
fighting? They eat together on Thanksgiving."

When Uncas shows up at Fort Saybrook and bestows
upon the English his offering of Pequot heads, Owen is outraged. He screams, "What?!"

Cut to the Pequot fort, where we have already seen a little
girl around Owen's age playing with a cornhusk doll while

being teased by her brother. The reenactor playing Captain Mason yells, "Burn them!" As the wigwams catch fire, Pequot kids are shrieking and holding on to their mothers. The English shoot at the Pequot who flee the flames. Horrified, Owen tugs my sleeve, demanding, "Aunt Sarah! When do they have Thanksgiving?"

"The one with the Pilgrims?" I whisper. "That happened sixteen years earlier."

Owen closes his eyes and refuses to watch the rest of the movie. When the lights go up, he asks his mother, "Who won?"

"The English," she replies.

One answer to Owen's question—When's Thanksgiving?—might be June 15, 1637. Winthrop writes in his journal that in Boston "There was a day of thanksgiving kept in all the churches for the victory obtained against the Pequot." To the Puritans, days of thanksgiving were not annual events. Days of thanksgiving were earned. They would be appalled by U.S. calendars calling for a holiday, Thanksgiving, with a capital T, on the fourth Thursday of November every year. What if we didn't deserve it? What if a day of fast was called for instead, days of fast being occasional days of punishment to repent for wayward collective behavior or as an act of prayer to call for God's help in precarious situations. In fact, Boston had held a fast the day before the massacre at Mystic, and Winthrop credits that one day's missed dinner for the resulting "general defeat of the Pequot." Thus did they earn the day of thanksgiving after the victory.

If the idea of putting on a picnic to celebrate seven hundred people being burned alive sounds crass, it was nevertheless not unheard of in the seventeenth century. In fact, during the English Civil War, when the Puritan Oliver Cromwell led his army to sack the Irish village of Drogheda on September 11, 1649, at least two thousand people died, including some who barricaded themselves inside a church that Cromwell set on fire, thus burning them alive like the Pequot in their fort. Cromwell prosecuted this holocaust in the same manner Captain Underhill applauded his men at Mystic—"without compassion." Though, according to Cromwell's biographer Antonia Fraser, "Oliver's own mercy was said to have been stirred by the sight of a tiny baby still trying hopelessly to feed from the breast of its dead mother." And what was the verdict on Drogheda back home in England? Fraser writes that the news was met with "delight and rejoicing. The ministers gave out the happy tidings from the pulpits; 30 October was set aside to be a day of public thanksgiving."

After the Mystic massacre movie ends, Amy and Owen and I leave the museum and repair to our nearby hotel, the Mohegan Sun Casino, operated by the Mohegan tribe. It looks like it was designed by Ralph Lauren, Bugsy Siegel, and Willy Wonka after a night of peyote. Which is to say that I kind of like it.

The registration desks are nestled under a half-dome, meant to evoke a wigwam. Inside, amidst the standard gambling accoutrements, like craps tables and slot machines, the building is done up in woven wood and birch bark. Support columns look like trees with candy-colored leaves. Murals depict Mohegan mythology. There's a display featuring a giant replica of Shantok cookware—the pottery associated with Uncas's nearby village—and it makes me wonder if four hundred years from now my nonstick frying pan will be made into a colossal sculpture for gamblers to admire. A charming statue of the late Mohegan anthropologist Gladys Tantaquidgeon is facing a sign that tallies up the "slot jackpot paid today." Uncas would undoubtedly get a kick out of his tribe presiding over such an impressive edifice built for the sole purpose of taking white people's wampum.

The three of us sit outside by the pool and Owen does a martial arts–influenced interpretive dance to Dick Dale's "Misirlou" while quizzing me on the story of the Pequot War.

"Don't tell me!" he says. "No, tell me."

I hit the highlights, starting with the Dutch murdering the Pequot chief and the Pequot avenging his death by mistakenly killing an Englishman and how the whole thing just kind of escalated into war. He says that sounds stupid. I say that most wars are. Then he asks me what state we're in.

"Connecticut," I tell him.

"And that war was here?" he asks.

Yes, I answer.

"Name a state where there was never a war," he says.

Flipping through various Indian skirmishes and the Civil War in my head, I reply, "I'm not sure I can."

"Then name a state where there was the least amount of war."

"I don't know," I say. "Idaho?" (I looked it up later; turns out I was unaware of the Battle of White Bird Canyon during the Nez Perce War.)

The next morning, we drive around in search of Uncas, walking around his headquarters, now Fort Shantok State Park. Then we drive to Norwich to look at Indian Leap, a chasm next to a waterfall where Uncas supposedly chased some Narragansett to their deaths in 1643.

"Was he trying to cut their heads off?" asks Owen.

No, I tell him. The sign says, "They plunged to their death into the abyss below."

In Norwich, we stop to look at the Uncas Monument, an obelisk, at the "Royal Mohegan Burial Ground." A plaque notes the monument was dedicated by President Andrew Jackson in 1833.

"Figures," my sister says. "One asshole honoring another." (For his Indian-removal policies Jackson is not remembered kindly by my family and our fellow Cherokee descendants.)

Amy and Owen can't get past Uncas decapitating those Pequot and taking part in the Mystic Massacre. Not that I find his behavior particularly uplifting, but I can understand the desperation behind Uncas's every lick of an English boot. He was ruthless in the pursuit of one goal, Mohegan survival. Standing in that cemetery, looking at the grave of Uncas's great-grandson, reading a plaque that states the Mohegan "descendants reside in Norwich today," it appears that Uncas succeeded in keeping his people intact and in proximity to the graves of their ancestors. What he did wasn't pretty. It wasn't even right. But it worked.

In a famous illustration from John Underhill's book on the Pequot War, the situation couldn't be more clear. Concentric circles depict the overwhelming force of the English and their allies surrounding the Pequot fort. The lesson? You're either burning or getting burnt.

We leave the Mohegan cemetery and stop off at the Mystic Aquarium to take a break from Indian troubles. But an exhibit devoted to algae living inside giant clams reminds me of Uncas's relationship with the English nonetheless.

In order to survive, giant clams and zooxanthella have adopted a mutualistic relationship (one that benefits both partners). Zooxanthella (plant-like algae) live inside giant clams to receive protection and a home. In turn zooxanthella provide the giant clam with the nutrients it needs to survive.

Obviously, the English are the clam and the Mohegan are the algae. If that analogy sounds unfair and one-sided and insulting to the Mohegan, that's because it is. Uncas simply decided that the only way to live was to live off the biggest giant clam around.

After the Pequot War, the Narragansett sachem Miantonomi took the exact opposite course of action from Uncas, with disastrous results. Horrified by the Mystic Massacre, Miantonomi could only conclude that the English were hellbent on native annihilation. So he set out to build a coalition of tribes to fight back, just as Tecumseh would at the turn of the nineteenth century.

In 1642, Lion Gardener, one of the officers from Fort Saybrook, was passing through Long Island when he witnessed a speech Miantonomi delivered to a local tribe.

He said:

> For so are we all Indians as the English are and say brother to one another; so must we be one as they are, otherwise we shall be all gone shortly. For you know our fathers had plenty of deer and skins, our plains were full of deer, as also our woods, and of turkeys, and our coves full of fish and fowl. But these English having gotten our land, they with scythes cut down the grass and with axes fell the trees; their cows and horses eat the grass, and their hogs spoil our clam banks, and we shall all be starved.

After enumerating his other Indian allies, he outlines a forthcoming plan of attack. He says, "And when you see the fires that will be made forty days hence in a clear night, then do as we, and the next day fall on and kill men, women, and children, but no cows, for they will serve to eat 'til our deer be increased again."

Miantonomi's speech foreshadows similar testimony among nineteenth-century American Indians such as Chief Seattle and Tecumseh himself, who would one day try and gather together allied Indian forces invoking the memory of what happened to the Pequot, whom he said had "vanished before the avarice and oppression of the white man, as snow before a summer sun."

When the English get wind of Miantonomi's plot, Massachusetts Bay Colony, Plymouth, and Connecticut form the United Colonies of New England, also called the New England Confederation, to officially act as a collective defensive alliance. (Roger Williams's heretical colony is purposefully left out of the coalition so Rhode Island's anything-goes cooties won't rub off on its proper, God-fearing neighbors.)

Meanwhile, Uncas captures Miantonomi and turns him over to the English authorities at Hartford. This prompts a secret meeting among representatives from the United Colonies to decide what to do about the prisoner. Winthrop reports in his journal that they conclude that "there was a general conspiracy among the Indians to cut off all the English and that Miantonomi was the head and contriver of it." Secondly, they agree that the Narragansett sachem "was of a turbulent and proud spirit, and would never be at rest."

They agree that Miantonomi should be assassinated, and

that Uncas is the man to do it. They send for him, and the Mohegan, according to Winthrop, "readily undertook the execution." Uncas orders his brother to carry out the task. Winthrop writes that Uncas's brother "clave [Miantonomi's] head with a hatchet, some English being present."

For the English, the Pequot War was a success ratified by God. It became the blueprint for all future Indian wars on the continent conducted by the colonists and the subsequent United States. The Mystic Massacre set a precedent. The mass murder of the Pequot made the mass murder of other tribes possible and therefore repeatable. It was the first of many similar horrors to come: the Bear River Massacre of the Shoshone in 1863 (after the U.S. Army killed a couple of hundred Shoshone men in battle, American soldiers allegedly raped the tribe's women and murdered children—which happened, with apologies to Owen, in Idaho); the Sand Creek Massacre in 1864 (in which the army slays almost two hundred Cheyenne); the Wounded Knee Massacre of 1890 (when the army gunned down nearly three hundred Lakota Sioux in the South Dakota snow).

Some U.S. Army veterans of the latter Lakota massacre, by the way, would then be dispatched by the McKinley administration to fight guerrilla warriors in the Philippines after we had won the islands from Spain, along with Cuba, Puerto Rico, and Guam, at the end of the Spanish-American War. That year, 1898, was the magic moment when the United States became a true world power, allowing previously isolationist America to return to its Puritan, come-over-and-help-us roots. Soon enough we were helping Europe in two world wars, helping South Korea, helping South Vietnam, just as we are now, as I write this, helping Iraq.

For Captain John Underhill, the co-architect of the Mystic Massacre, having commanded the soldiers who decimated the Pequot was not enough to sustain his hero's welcome back in Boston. He was a friend of the trouble-maker Anne Hutchinson. To the General Court, no amount of Pequot blood could wash off the stain of her beliefs. Underhill was forced to flee the colony he had so stalwartly, and so cruelly, defended.

A nne Marbury Hutchinson, her husband, William, and their whopping brood of fifteen children arrive in Boston on September 18, 1634. In Winthrop's diary, he notes the arrival of their ship, the *Griffin,* but not the Hutchinsons themselves. Later on, he would call Will Hutchinson "a man of a very mild temper and weak parts, and wholly guided by his wife."

Anne herself is guided by John Cotton. Cotton is why they're here. Back in England, the Hutchinsons used to travel routinely over twenty miles just to hear him preach. Anne is Cotton's groupie, and after he emigrates to America she soon packs up her family and follows.

And hers is one large family. Anne and Will Hutchinson

have fifteen children. The daughter of a persecuted Puritan minister who helped her cobble together the best education possible for female children (who were denied university attendance), Anne Hutchinson is one of the brainiest Englishwomen of the seventeenth century. Yet she is no stranger to the goopy fluids of female biology. Besides birthing her own litter, she works as a midwife, delivering babies and no doubt serving the brew imbibed before and after labor, the wonderfully named "groaning beer."

By aiding Boston's new mothers, Hutchinson quickly befriends a lot of women. She starts leading the women in a regular Bible study in her large, fine home. (Her husband might be whipped but he sure is rich.) At first, they simply discuss Cotton's latest sermon.

Unfortunately, Hutchinson didn't write down or publish any of her commentaries. She suffers the same fate in the historical record as the Pequot; her thoughts and deeds have been passed down to us solely through the writings of white men who pretty much hate her guts.

A ladies' study group is one of the most ubiquitous social subsets in the history of Christian churches. I attended one regularly with my mother as a child. Once, when I told a member of the fabled East Coast Media Elite that I was raised Pentecostal he asked if that meant I grew up "fondling snakes in trailers." I replied, "You know that book club you're in? Well, my church was a lot like that, except we actually read the book."

Anne Hutchinson is hosting more than a ladies' study group. Dozens and dozens of Bostonians come to her home to hear her preach. Men start coming, too. And not just any old men—young Governor Henry Vane himself. She has something other people want, some combination of confidence and glamour and hope. She is the Puritan Oprah—a leader, a guru, a star.

Hutchinson, still swooning, spiritually speaking, for Cotton, nevertheless starts departing from her mentor's lectures and lets rip her own opinions and beliefs.

One person keeping an eye on her, both theologically and literally, is John Winthrop, who lives across the street. (The site of her home would later house Ticknor and Fields, the famous book publisher of Ralph Waldo Emerson, Henry David Thoreau, Harriet Beecher Stowe, and, appropriately, Nathaniel Hawthorne, who, in *The Scarlet Letter*'s first chapter, misspells her first name but nevertheless honors Hutchinson by describing a rose bush in bloom said to have "sprung up under the footsteps of the sainted Ann Hutchinson, as she entered the prison door" and symbolizing "some sweet moral blossom." Nowadays, the place is a jewelry store. Last time I walked by it there were Canadian diamonds in the window with necklaces displayed next to photos of grazing caribou, grazing caribou apparently being a Canadian girl's best friend.)

On October 21, 1636, Winthrop writes in his journal, "One Mrs. Hutchinson, a member of the church of Boston, a woman of a ready wit and bold spirit, brought over with her two dangerous errors." Her first error, he says, is the belief "that the person of the Holy Ghost dwells in a justified person." Puritan orthodoxy prefers to think of said Holy Ghost as hanging around next to a person who has been saved—kind of like a garden-variety ghost, actually. Winthrop will later explain this with the analogy of a marriage: in "a union . . . as between husband and wife, he is a man still, and she a woman." As opposed to Hutchinson's version, in which the spirit dwells within, *Invasion of the Body Snatchers* style.

As Edmund S. Morgan writes in *The Puritan Dilemma,* Hutchinson's notion of the Holy Ghost living inside a believer "was dangerously close to a belief in immediate personal revelation." Earlier, when I was trying to point out that the Puritans of Massachusetts Bay Colony had little in common with present-day evangelical Christians, this is what I meant. Hutchinson's emphasis on "immediate personal revelation"—radical at the time—is now a core value of many American Protestant sects, including the Pentecostal one I was raised in.

For example, my family attended church three times a week. Once, when I was around eight, I complained about having to go to the Wednesday-night sermon because sometimes it went late and I wanted to get home in time to watch my favorite TV show, *Charlie's Angels.* Granted, that program's teachings were often at odds with the teachings of the Wednesday-night sermon, which my mother discovered to her horror when my Barbie started ordering a green cock-tail called a "grasshopper" and climbing into bed with Ken, whom she refused to marry because she was more interested in her career.

Anyway, I remember whining, "Why do we have to go to church?"

My mother answered, "We don't *have* to go church."

"Great!" I said.

"We *are* going to church," she said. She said we go there "for fellowship" and to learn and pray. But she also said that all one needs to be saved is to believe in Jesus and accept him into your heart. Then she quoted John 3:16: "For God so loved the world, that he gave his only begotten Son, that whosoever believeth in him should not perish, but have everlasting life."

From the perspective of catching the beginning of *Charlie's Angels,* her saying we were still going to church was bad news. But the rest of what she said was a source of self-determination and responsibility all at once. What I took from this revelation was that no one else was responsible for my salvation—that no church, no preacher, not even the Bible, come to think of it, had power over me. My highest authority was the spiritual presence within.

Compare that to standard theological procedure in Massachusetts Bay. Hutchinson's creed—like my mother's, of privileging a personal relationship with God over everything else—writes Morgan, "threatened the fundamental conviction on which the Puritans built their state, their churches, and their daily lives, namely that God's will could be discovered only through the Bible"—a Bible dissected and interpreted by two ordained ministers, the teacher and the pastor, in church services with mandatory attendance.

Hutchinson's second error, according to Winthrop, is that according to her, "no sanctification can help to evidence to us our justification." In other words, she rejects the Puritan conclusion that a member of the Elect is a visible saint who seems like a member of the Elect.

Hutchinson and her accusers would agree that one of the basic gists of Puritanism is an argument against a covenant of works, which is to say Puritanism denies everything that's nice and comforting about Catholicism. Giving alms to the poor? Confessing one's sins to a priest who suggests the sinner repeat prayers memorized by rote—the "Hail Mary," for instance—and then feeling better? None of that for the Puritans. Oh, every Puritan is welcome, even required, to do good and be good and show up at church and help the needy—the Bible tells them so. But those actions alone do not admit a believer into heaven. Only God does that, through the grace of His salvation, hence the name covenant of grace. Which, as we have noted, God only doles out to a select few individuals, none of whom are ever entirely certain they have made the cut.

The difference between Anne Hutchinson and her accusers is that Hutchinson believes that anyone, even a nonbeliever, can *seem* saved. The only way to know one is saved is when one *feels* saved. Puritans, however, are suspicious of feelings, especially the feelings of a woman without proper theological training from Cambridge University.

"There joined with her in these opinions," Winthrop writes, "a brother of hers, one Mr. Wheelwright, a silenced minister sometimes in England." The fate of John Wheelwright, who is married to Hutchinson's sister, is entwined with Hutchinson's, partly because he and Cotton are the only clergymen Hutchinson approves of, the only ministers she condones for preaching about the covenant of grace instead of the covenant of works. The other reason Wheelwright is caught up in the momentum of Hutchinson's controversy with the Bay Colony officials is that she inspires her followers to demand that Wheelwright be put on the payroll as a minister of the Boston church.

That is Winthrop's own congregation. On October 30, 1636, he writes in his journal, "Some of the church of Boston, being of the opinion of Mrs. Hutchinson, had labored to have Mr. Wheelwright to be called to be a teacher there. . . . One of the church stood up and said, he could not consent."

This anonymous "one" was most likely Winthrop himself, who goes on to describe the man's reasoning: "because the church being well furnished already with able ministers, whose spirits they knew, and whose labors God had blessed in much love and sweet peace." I.e., they've got Cotton, they've got Wilson; so, minister-wise, they're all set. Wheelwright, however, is still well within the traditional Bostonian being-talked-out-of-one's-questionable-opinions grace period, and it is suggested that perhaps he could lead a congregation in nearby Braintree.

The word Winthrop uses to characterize Hutchinson and Wheelwright's thought is "antinomian," which means "against the law." This period is often called by historians the "Antinomian Controversy." Winthrop, as a magistrate, is on the side of the law.

Like a lot of Puritan disagreements, this one is tricky. Winthrop is by no means opposed to the covenant of grace. He actually shares Hutchinson's admiration for Cotton, and nurturing the covenant of grace is Cotton's specialty. Recall that Winthrop praised Cotton for having such a talent for waking lackluster believers from spiritual slumber that the Boston church underwent a boom of enthusiasm after Cotton came to town. Even Winthrop, in the middle of the Antinomian Controversy, admitted to such an awakening, calling it "the voice of peace."

Anne Hutchinson is merely taking Protestantism's next logical step. If Protestantism is an evolutionary process devoted to the ideal of getting closer and closer to God, it starts with doing away with Latin-speaking popes and bishops in favor of locally elected but nevertheless highly educated, ordained clergymen, and Bibles translated into the believers' mother tongues. This is the "New England Way."

Hutchinson is pushing American Protestantism further, toward a practice approaching the more personal, ecstatic, anti-intellectual, emotional slant now practiced in the U.S.A., especially in the South and Midwest. We call that swath of geography the "Bible Belt," but that would have been a more accurate description of bookish seventeenth-century New England. While modern evangelicals obviously set store in the Bible, their partiality for alone time with their deity means that a truer name for what we now call the Bible Belt might be something along the lines of the Personal Relationship with Jesus Christ Belt, or the Filled with the Holy Spirit Basket of America.

Protestantism's evolution away from hierarchy and authority has enormous consequences for America and the world. On the one hand, the democratization of religion runs parallel to political democratization. The king of England, questioning the pope, inspires English subjects to question the king and his Anglican bishops. Such dissent is backed up by a Bible full of handy Scripture arguing for arguing with one's king. This is the root of self-government in the English-speaking world.

On the other hand, Protestantism's shedding away of authority, as evidenced by my mother's proclamation that I needn't go to church or listen to a preacher to achieve salvation, inspires self-reliance—along with a dangerous disregard for expertise. So the impulse that leads to democracy can also be the downside of democracy—namely, a suspicion of people who know what they are talking about. It's why in U.S. presidential elections the American people will elect a wisecracking good ol' boy who's fun in a malt shop instead of a serious thinker who actually knows some of the pompous, brainy stuff that might actually get fewer people laid off or killed.

By December of 1636, tensions between the two factions of Hutchinson/Wheelwright versus Winthrop/Wilson (with John Cotton in the middle), take their toll on at least one Bostonian. Winthrop writes in his journal that at a meeting of the magistrates, Henry Vane claims he needs to resign as governor and return to England for "reasons concerning his own estate," the seventeenth-century version of a politician's resignation made in the name of spending more time with his family. As this is "a time of such danger" due to the ongoing Indian troubles, Vane's colleagues chew him out for even considering abandoning a colony in need. He agrees to stick around, but he complains of foreseeing "God's judgments to come upon us for these differences and dissensions, which he saw amongst us." Then Winthrop writes that Vane "brake forth into tears."

In earlier paragraphs devoted to the Pequot War, I have mentioned that Winthrop records that on January 20, 1637, "a general fast was kept in all the churches," a punishment meant to appeal to God to help the colony with its Indian troubles and "the dissensions of our churches."

John Cotton preaches a Fast Day sermon meant to scold

the colonists for their bickering. He quotes from Isaiah 58:4: "Behold, ye fast for strife and debate." Then, John Wheelwright asks to preach and, in the spirit of reconciliation, Cotton lets him.

"The only cause of fasting of true believers," remarks Wheelwright, "is the absence of Christ." This is a serious accusation. Remember that in Winthrop's "Model of Christian Charity," of seven years earlier, he supposed that in New England, God "will delight to dwell among us as His own people." But Wheelwright continues that if Christ "be present with his people, then they have no cause to fast."

Then Wheelwright, clearly alluding to his and Hutchinson's beleaguered little faction, proclaims that "the saints of God are few, they are but a little flock." Then, alluding to Winthrop's side, he continues, "Those that are enemies to the Lord, not only paganish, but antichristian, and those that run under a covenant of works are very strong."

With this sermon, Winthrop writes, Wheelwright "stirred up the people . . . with much bitterness and vehemency." Hutchinson's followers start "frequenting the lectures of other ministers" to "make much disturbance by public questions, and objections to their doctrines." Thus the Hutchinsonians from Boston become an irreverent peanut gallery, traveling the colony to interrupt the sermons of other towns' ministers. Such outrageous questioning of authority is an obvious violation of the Fifth Commandment, as it dishonors church fathers.

At the next meeting of the General Court, Winthrop writes that Wheelwright is found "guilty of sedition, and also of contempt, for that the court had appointed the fast as a means of reconciliation of the differences . . . and he purposefully set himself to kindle and increase them."

Vane, who is still governor at the start of the meeting, protests in vain. Wheelwright's sentencing is postponed until the next court in May, though it will be postponed again. By the end of the meeting, Winthrop is reelected governor, which is a rebuke of Vane, and, by extension, of Wheelwright and Hutchinson.

Also in May 1637 the court issues an order, writes Winthrop, "to keep out all such persons as might be dangerous to the commonwealth." And who will be the arbiters of which persons are or are not dangerous? The magistrates, of course. This outrageous immigration policy is meant expressly to bar the Hutchinson and Wheelwright camp from importing supporters to their cause. Vane, who was voted out as governor but remains as one of the deputies (and one of Anne Hutchinson's best friends), is infuriated by this policy. After Winthrop defends it, Vane writes in response, "This law we judge to be most wicked and sinful." Among his objections to the law, Vane includes the fact that it gives the power "to expel and reject those which are most eminent Christians, if they suit not with the disposition of the magistrates." Vane's point is dangerously close to Roger Williams's recognition that Christianity is inherently divisive and when it is the state religion, the Christians in power tend to persecute other kinds of Christians with whom they disagree. One of Vane's more basic, and legally correct, arguments against the law is that it could theoretically bar the king himself from setting foot in this part of his own kingdom. Which is a violation of the Charter's charge for the colonists to make no law "repugnant to the laws of England."

The Bay Colony's reactionary immigration legislation is not unlike reactionary immigration legislation throughout history: it exposes a people's deepest fears. For example, the Anarchist Exclusion Act of 1903, passed by Congress to bar anarchists from the United States after an anarchist assassinated President McKinley. Or the not particularly Magna Carta–friendly clause in the USA Patriot Act of 2001 allowing for illegal immigrants to be detained indefinitely and without legal counsel for up to six months if they are suspected of terrorism, or simply have terrorist "ties."

Behind every bad law, a deep fear. And in 1637, the two things panicking the leaders of the Massachusetts Bay Colony the most are the Pequot and Anne Hutchinson. After the Pequot are burned alive in May, Winthrop and his fellow magistrates have one down and one to go.

In August, Vane sails home to England for good. It must have been a relief to go where an Englishman is generally allowed to just show up unannounced, without court approval.

In the years to come, Vane will stand out as a rare man during the English Civil War, an actual moderate. He is in the minority of Puritan Members of Parliament who argue against beheading Charles I, writing later that the king's execution "will be questioned whether that was an act of justice or murder." ("The most interesting thing about King Charles I," reports Monty Python, "is that he was 5 foot 6 inches tall at the start of his reign, but only 4 foot 8 inches tall at the end of it.")

Vane's friend Oliver Cromwell had commanded his army to defeat a king in the name of Parliament only to then make himself Lord Protector and dissolve Parliament like the king before him. Vane becomes such an outspoken critic of Cromwell's despotism that Cromwell is said to have cried, "The Lord deliver me from thee, Henry Vane!"

Forced to retire from public life during Cromwell's dictatorship, Vane takes to writing. Like Roger Williams, Vane believes in religious liberty, gently insisting that when freedom of worship is denied, people "are nourished up in a biting, devouring, wrathful spirit, one against another, and are found transgressors of that royal law which forbids us to do that unto another which we would not have them do unto us." In other words, required membership in one religion, like that in Massachusetts Bay, is a violation of the golden rule called for by Jesus, the King of Kings, in the Sermon on the Mount.

When Cromwell's weakling son Richard tries to hold on to his father's title, Vane writes a withering summary of the whole country's misgivings about Richard's character, stating:

One could bear a little with Oliver Cromwell, though, contrary to his oath of fidelity to the Parliament, contrary to his duty to the public, contrary to the respect he owed that venerable body from whom he received his authority, he usurped the government. His merit was so extraordinary, that our judgments, our passions might be blinded by it. He made his way to empire by the most illustrious actions; he had under his command an army that had made him conqueror, and a people that had made him their general. But, as for Richard Cromwell, his son, who is he? What are his titles? We have seen that he had a sword by his side; but did he ever draw it? And what is of more importance in this case, is he fit to get obedience from a mighty nation, who could never make a footman obey him? Yet, we must recognize this man as our king, under the style of protector!—a man without birth, without courage, without conduct! For my part, I declare, sir, it shall never be said that I made such a man my master!

Such talk paved the way for the return of Charles II, the dead king's son, from exile in France. After Charles II came home to England and the monarchy was restored, the new king condemned to death a few men he held responsible for the execution of his father, including Henry Vane. Who had argued against the execution! Vane was beheaded. (Cromwell was, too—posthumously. Charles II had Cromwell's corpse dug up, dragged through the streets of London, hanged on a gallows, taken down, and decapitated. His rotting head was skewered on a pike and displayed at Westminster for over twenty years. Eventually, Cromwell's skull was buried at his old college in Cambridge.)

Henry Vane's headless ghost is said to haunt the library of his father's house, Raby Castle. But I think it's more accurate to say that Vane's departure in 1637 haunts American history. I can't help but wonder what might have been had he stuck around and lived out his years in New England as John Winthrop's conscience instead of Oliver Cromwell's. Vane's later writing has much in common with the Winthrop of "Christian Charity." In his book *The Retired Man's Meditations,* Vane describes a good society, in Winthrop-like terms, as "reunited of all good men as one man in a happy union of their spirits, prayers and counsels, to resist all common danger . . . and promote the interest and common welfare of the whole."

Reading those words, Vane's abandonment of New England can be seen as the Massachusetts Bay Colony's loss. Vane was a person—a governor—who possessed Williams's insistence on religious liberty *and* Winthrop's beautiful communitarian ideals (but without his totalitarian flaws). Vane was so young in Massachusetts that the disagreements of other men made him cry like a girl. But he matured into a formidable advocate for goodwill and common sense. Considering what happened to his friend Anne Hutchinson right after his exit, Massachusetts could have used him.

I n September of 1637, one month after Henry Vane sailed away, the freemen meet to decide on matters Hutchinsonian. They resolve, writes Winthrop, "That though women might meet (some few together) to pray and edify one another," assemblies of "sixty or more" as were then taking place in Boston at the home of "one woman" who had had the gall to go about "resolving questions of doctrine and expounding scripture" are not allowed. The Bill of Rights, with its allowance for freedom of assembly, is a long way off.

Also, a member of a church's congregation "might ask a question publicly, after sermon, for information; yet this ought to be very wisely and sparingly done." In other words, no heckling the ministers allowed.

In November, Wheelwright appears before the court and, refusing to repent for his Fast Day sermon the previous January, is, Winthrop writes, "disenfranchised and banished." So are four other supporters of Hutchinson and Wheelwright, including John Underhill, hero of the Mystic Massacre.

"The court also sent for Mrs. Hutchinson," writes Winthrop, "and charged her with . . . keeping two public lectures every week in her house," which were attended by "sixty to eighty persons." She is also accused of "reproaching most of the ministers," except for Cotton, "for not preaching a covenant of free grace, and that they had not the seal of the spirit."

Hutchinson's judges are Winthrop, Deputy Governor Thomas Dudley, five assistants, and five deputies. Various ministers, including John Cotton, are also present. As governor, Winthrop presides over the trial, for the most part stupidly. Hutchinson continually outwits him, even though she is, at the age of forty-six, pregnant yet again.

Winthrop explains to Hutchinson she has been "called here as one of those that have troubled the peace of the commonwealth." And, as is his policy toward all godly persons who repent their blunders, he offers the court's corrections, so that she "may become a profitable member here among us." If not, "the court may take such course that you may trouble us no further."

Hutchinson points out she has not been charged with anything. Winthrop says he just told her why she's here.

"What have I said or done?" she asks.

Winthrop answers that she "did harbor . . . parties in this faction that you have heard of." I.e., she invited troublemakers into her home.

Then he accuses her of being in favor of Wheelwright's Fast Day sermon, and those in favor of the sermon "do break a law."

"What law have I broken?" she asks.

"Why the fifth commandment," answers Winthrop. This is of course the favorite commandment of all ministers and magistrates, the one demanding a person should honor his father and mother, which for Winthrop includes all authority figures. Wheelwright's sermon was an affront to the fathers of the church and the fathers of the commonwealth.

A Ping-Pong match follows in which Winthrop accuses her of riling up Wheelwright's faction and she's, like, "What faction?" And he accuses her of having "counseled" this mysterious faction and she wonders how she did that and he answers, "Why in entertaining them."

She asks him to cite the law against having people over. And he lamely says she has broken the law of "dishonoring the commonwealth."

(Genealogy buffs might enjoy learning that this lopsided battle of the wits will be repeated between Winthrop and Hutchinson's descendants during the presidential debates of 2004. Winthrop's heir, John Kerry, debates Hutchinson's great-something grandson, George W. Bush. Only in this instance it's the Hutchinson who is flummoxed by his opponent's sensical answers. Bush's constant blinking appears on television as if he thinks the answers to the questions he's being asked are tattooed inside his own eyelids.)

Winthrop and Hutchinson go back and forth as to whether or not she's honoring her parents, and Winthrop is so flummoxed by the way she crushes his shaky arguments, he erupts, "We do not mean to discourse with those of your sex." Not a particularly good comeback, considering that they're the ones who have forced her into this discourse.

He then quizzes her on why she holds her commonwealth-dishonoring meetings at her house. She cites Paul's

Epistle to Titus, in the New Testament, which calls for "the elder women" to "instruct the younger."

He tells her that what she's supposed to instruct the younger women on is "to love their husbands and not to make them clash."

She responds, "If any come to my house to be instructed in the ways of God what rule have I to put them away?"

"Your opinions," Winthrop claims, "may seduce many simple souls that resort unto you." Furthermore, with all these women at Hutchinson's house instead of their own, "Families should be neglected for so many neighbors and dames and so much time spent."

When she presses him once again to point out the Scripture that contradicts the Scripture she has quoted calling for elders to mentor younger women, Winthrop, flustered, barks, "We are your judges, and not you ours."

Winthrop really is no match for Hutchinson's logic. Most of his answers to her challenges boil down to "Because I said so."

In fact, before this trial started, the colony's elders had agreed to raise four hundred pounds to build a college but hadn't gotten around to doing anything about it. After Hutchinson's trial, they got cracking immediately and founded Harvard so as to prevent random, home-schooled female maniacs from outwitting magistrates in open court and seducing colonists, even male ones, into strange opinions. Thanks in part to Hutchinson, the young men of Massachusetts will receive a proper, orthodox theological education grounded in the rigorous study of Hebrew and Greek.

Moving along, Winthrop asks her of ministers preaching "a covenant of works, do they preach truth?"

"Yes sir," she answers, "but when they preach a covenant of works for salvation, that is not truth." In other words, it's fine to exhort people to good behavior, but good behavior is not going to save their souls. Which is in fact, what every person in the room, including Winthrop, believes. They are angry with her because she has accused all the ministers except for Cotton and her brother-in-law, Wheelwright, of preaching *only* a covenant of works, a Puritan put-down. Several ministers then gang up on her to claim that that's what she's been going around saying.

The trial resumes the next morning and John Cotton is called to testify. If the court can get the beloved Cotton, Hutchinson's highest-ranking friend, to rat her out for heresy or sedition, she's lost. He stands by her, though, more or less. He says he regrets that any comparison has been made between him and his colleagues, calling it "uncomfortable." But, he adds, "I must say that I did not find her saying that they were under a covenant of works, nor that she said they did preach a covenant of works."

Cotton has exonerated her. Now the court has to acquit her. And it would have except that one person stands up and gives the testimony that will get Anne Hutchinson banished from Massachusetts. And that person is: Anne Hutchinson.

"If you please to give me leave I shall give you the ground of what I know to be true," she says.

Music to John Winthrop's ears. He was about to step in and silence her. But, while the trial transcript proves that she's a better debater than he, he's no idiot. He later recalls, "Perceiving whereabouts she went"—namely, self-incrimination—he "permitted her to proceed."

I wish I didn't understand why Hutchinson risks damning herself to exile and excommunication just for the thrill of shooting off her mouth and making other people listen up. But this here book is evidence that I have this confrontational, chatty bent myself. I got my first radio job when I was eighteen years old and I've been yakking on air or in print ever since. Hutchinson is about to have her life—and her poor family's—turned upside down just so she can indulge in the sort of smart-alecky diatribe for which I've gotten paid for the last twenty years.

Hutchinson starts by informing the court of her spiritual biography. She recalls that back home, she was disconcerted by the "falseness" of the Church of England and contemplated "turn[ing] Separatist." But after a "day of solemn humiliation," she had, like every man in the room, decided against separatism. Unlike every man in the room, she claimed to hear the voice of God, who "let me see which was the clear ministry and which the wrong." Ever since, she continues, she has been hearing voices—Moses, John the Baptist, even "the voice of Antichrist."

To the men before her (and, by the way, to me) this is
crazy talk. It might also be devil talk. An assistant asks her,
"How do you know that was the spirit?"

Her answer couldn't be more uppity. She compares herself to the most exalted Hebrew patriarch facing the Bible's
most famous spiritual dilemma: "How did Abraham know
that it was God that bid him offer his son, being a breach of
the sixth commandment?"

Dudley replies, "By an immediate voice."

Hutchinson: "So to me by an immediate revelation . . . by
the voice of his own spirit to my soul."

This is blasphemous enough, but she's on a roll. She then
dares them to mess with her, a woman who has the entire
Holy Trinity on speed dial. "Look what you do," she warns.
"You have power over my body but the Lord Jesus hath power
over my body and soul." Their lies, she claims, "will bring a
curse upon you and your posterity, and the mouth of the
Lord hath spoken it."

Winthrop provokes her further. Since she is shameless
enough to compare herself to Abraham, he seems to think it
might be fun to find out if she is Daniel in the lion's den,
too. "Daniel was delivered by miracle," he says. "Do you
think to be delievered so too?"

Yep. "I do here speak it before the court," she responds
helpfully, adding, "I look that the Lord should deliver me by
his providence." She claims God told her, "'I am the same

God that delivered Daniel out of the lion's den, I will also deliver thee.'"

She was quoting God. Not the Bible. Just something God said to her one day when they were hanging out.

A magistrate named William Bartholomew who had sailed to Massachusetts on the *Griffin* with Hutchinson pipes up that when Boston came into view she was alarmed by "the meanness of the place" but then proclaimed that "if she had not a sure word that England should be destroyed, her heart would shake." Bartholomew recalls that "it seemed to me at that time very strange and witchlike that she should say so."

Hutchinson denies Bartholomew's claim. When Winthrop presses him further, Bartholomew says that back in England he heard her profess "that she had never had any great thing done about her but it was revealed to her beforehand." In other words, she claimed to be able to predict the future. Hutchinson denies this as well.

Now that her witchlike pronouncements are on the table, Deputy Governor Thomas Dudley shrewdly seizes the opportunity to challenge John Cotton as to whether "you approve of Mistress Hutchinson's revelations."

Cotton is stuck. Hutchinson has handily enumerated her shocking delusions of grandeur. She has claimed to hear the voice of God. Honorable men have testified that she boasts of being able to predict the future. The disquieting syllable "witch" has come up. On the one hand, this woman has been his friend and stalwart supporter for years. On the other hand, if he sticks up for her, he could end up like Wheelwright and Underhill and the other men who have defended her—banished. And Cotton already knows what that's like, remembers well his time back in England on the run from Bishop Laud, hiding out in friends' houses, his wife being followed, unable to practice his calling. When he went underground, he was a man without a home or a church, which to an old preacher like Cotton is the same thing.

Dudley presses him: "Do you believe her revelations are true?"

Winthrop steps in, saying, "I am persuaded that the revelation she brings forth is delusion." There's a surprise.

Finally, in one sentence, Cotton sells out Hutchinson by recalling hearing another of her claims to predict the future. He says, "I remember she said she should be delivered by God's providence, whether now or at another time she knew not."

In this context, Cotton's concession is a smoking gun. He doesn't elaborate. He doesn't have to.

Winthrop is ready to take a vote:

Mrs. Hutchinson for these things that appear before us is unfit for our society, and if it be the mind of the court that she shall be banished out of our liberties and imprisoned till she be sent away, let them hold up their hands.

Nine out of twelve hands go up, among them, of course, Winthrop's. He continues, "Mrs. Hutchinson, the sentence of the court you hear is that you are banished from out of our jurisdiction as being a woman not fit for our society, and are to be imprisoned till the court shall send you away."

She demands, "I desire to know wherefore I am banished?"

Winthrop waves her off. "Say no more," he commands. "The court knows wherefore and is satisfied."

In the *Short Story of the Rise, Reign, and Ruin of the Antinomians, and Libertines that Infected the Churches of New England,* a victory tract published in London in 1644 and almost certainly written by Winthrop, Hutchinson is famously described as "this American Jezebel" whose downfall came when "the hand of civil justice laid hold on her, and then she began evidently to decline, and the faithful to be freed from her forgeries."

After being banished by the court, Hutchinson is excommunicated by the church. Winthrop writes in his diary that though her banishment had left her "somewhat dejected," excommunication cheered her up. "She gloried in her sufferings, saying that it was the greatest happiness, next to Christ, that ever befell her." He adds that it's actually the churches of Massachusetts that are happiest, as the "poor souls who had been seduced by her" had "settled again in the truth."

Winthrop writes that Hutchinson went "by land to Providence, and so to the island in the Narragansett Bay," that being Aquidneck, currently called Rhode Island. There, with the help of her fellow banishee, Roger Williams, Hutchinson, her husband, their litter of children, and some of her followers settled on land "purchased of the Indians." There they would found the town of Portsmouth.

Soon after her departure, it comes to Winthrop's attention that back in Hutchinson's Boston midwifery days, she and a fellow midwife had delivered the stillborn baby of her friend Mary Dyer and, with the blessing of John Cotton, secretly buried the fetus. The reason for this cover-up, according to Winthrop, was "that the child was a monster."

When the other midwife is interrogated by a church elder she confesses that the child, a girl, "had a face, but no head, and the ears stood upon the shoulders and were like an ape's; it had no forehead, but over the eyes four horns, hard and sharp." Also, her "nose hooked upward," her back was covered in scales, "it had two mouths" and "instead of toes, it had on each foot three claws, like a young fowl, with sharp talons."

For a woman, it can't get any worse than bearing a stillborn child, right? Oh, but it can, especially for a woman living in the Massachusetts Bay Colony. Remember that to the Puritans, all luck, good or bad, is a message from God, and thus deserved. A stillborn child is to be seen as God's punishment of the parents. A stillborn "monster" was obviously an even harsher divine judgment.

Winthrop queried Cotton as to why he advised the women to hide this deformity. The minister answered simply in the terms of the golden rule, that if the girl had been his own child, "he should have desired to have had it concealed." Also, he had witnessed other "monstrous births" and had concluded that these punishments from God were meant solely "for the instruction of the parents."

Winthrop convinces Cotton that the parents of monstrous stillborns are supposed to be a cautionary tale to others—other sinners. And according to Winthrop, Cotton makes a public apology, "which was well accepted."

If only that were the end of this grisly business. Winthrop, after seeking the advice of the other magistrates and church elders, gives orders for Mary Dyer's stillborn child to be exhumed. John Winthrop, who once said those beautiful words to his shipmates about mourning and suffering together, dug up what he thought was a decomposing monster—a monster sent as a message from God that Anne Hutchinson was wrong. The fetus, he writes in his journal, was "much corrupted, yet most of those things were to be seen, as the horns and claws, the scales, etc."

The only monster in this anecdote is Winthrop. He explains the child's death as a consequence of her mother's friendship with Anne Hutchinson. To him, this is vindication. The obvious enjoyment he gets out of recounting how mere proximity to Anne Hutchinson destroyed Mary Dyer's child is surpassed only by his glee a few months later when he hears the news from Rhode Island that Anne Hutchinson herself had "expected deliverance of a child" but "was delivered of a monstrous birth" instead. He even goes so far as to write a doctor he knows living on Aquidneck, fishing for juicy details about the fetus.

Then, just as he wrote they should in "Christian Charity," Winthrop and his Boston congregation rejoice together. In his journal, he writes that John Cotton celebrates the death of Hutchinson's fetus in his next sermon, proclaiming it to "signify her error in denying inherent righteousness" and that "all Christ was in us." Winthrop had predicted in "Christian Charity" that God "will delight to dwell among us as His own people" and this had come to pass.

Winthrop won. As a good Calvinist, he will continue to write in his journal things like "the devil would never cease to disturb our peace." But still, by 1638, the troublemakers were gone. Williams had been banished and yet still served as Winthrop's toady in dealing with the Indians. Hutchinson was not only banished but giving birth to the monster babies she deserved in godforsaken Rhode Island. The Pequot were done for. That swanky crybaby Henry Vane had sniffled his way back to England, and Winthrop with his God-given tallness was governor again. Even the ship that was supposed to bring a new governor commissioned by Archbishop Laud had literally broken apart—'twas by God's providence, for sure. And anyway, the king had so many

problems back home as the English Civil War starts to sim-
mer, he couldn't be bothered about a few scruffy religious
fanatics in Massachusetts.

When Winthrop first mentioned the tiny, ragged settlement of Boston in his journal in 1630, it was to record that a
goat had died. Back then, every goat seemed to count. When
he died in 1649, even if Boston had yet to become that city
upon a hill he'd dreamed of, it was a city nonetheless. Today,
from his grave, near John Cotton's, in the King's Chapel
Burying Ground, you can look across noisy Tremont Street at
a bland, concrete office building, a perfect stereotype of cap-
italist efficiency.

Such architectural stability would no doubt please Winthrop. But not this: around the corner, on Beacon Street, the
grounds of the Massachusetts State House feature statues of
heroes from the history of the commonwealth. There are
two bronze representatives from Winthrop's era—Anne
Hutchinson and Mary Dyer.

M ary Dyer and her husband were among Anne
Hutchinson's followers who were banished from
the Massachusetts Bay Colony and followed her to Portsmouth, Rhode Island. Later, on a trip to England, Mary will
convert to Quakerism and return to Massachusetts in 1658
to preach against the colony's new law banning Quakers.

They banish her again. When she returns a third time, she is arrested, sentenced to death, and hanged on Boston Common, which is across the street from her mournful but elegant statue on the State House grounds.

In Portsmouth, Hutchinson and Dyer are remembered in a park called Founders Brook, a lovely spot next to a little stream under the shade of old trees. Hutchinson and Dyer are each remembered on plaques attached to rocks, Hutchinson's talking her up as a "wife, mother, midwife, visionary, spiritual leader and original settler."

Near these rocks, plantings of echinacea, hollyhock, and fennel grow. A feminine hand has written "Hutchinson-Dyer Women's Healing Garden" in black marker on a small piece of plywood. I wish I could say that I find comfort in the words "women's healing garden." I like gardens and healing and quite a few women. I drink echinacea tea and enjoy fennel in salads. I even have a concrete casting of an abstract hollyhock designed by Frank Lloyd Wright hanging on my living room wall.

That said, the words "women's healing garden" fill me with the same feminist dread I feel when a subscription card falls out of a magazine and I catch a glimpse at the address form. A potential male magazine subscriber is given the choice of one title, "Mr.," but a female magazine subscriber is given three choices, thereby requiring a woman to inform perfect strangers in the mail room at *Newsweek* or Condé Nast exactly what kind of woman she is. She is either male property (Mrs.), wannabe male property (Miss), or man-hating harpy (Ms.).

I hate that I'm picking on a nice little flower garden planted by well-intentioned, historically minded horticulturalists. I guess the Women's Healing Garden makes me uncomfortable for the same reason I feel for Anne Hutchinson—because it's unfair that her gender kept her from pursuing her calling. She should have been a minister or a magistrate. She should have had John Cotton's job—or John Winthrop's. Instead, she spent her working life brewing groaning beer and burying deformed fetuses in the dead of night. There's nothing wrong with healing women, or women's healing. There is something very wrong, or at least very sad, that a legal, theological mind like hers, on display only in her trial transcripts, didn't get to study law or divinity at Cambridge like her male peers and accusers. As Peter G. Gomes once wrote in an article in Harvard's alumni magazine about Hutchinson's role in the origins of that institution, "Inadvertent midwife to a college founded in part to protect posterity from her errors, Anne Marbury Hutchinson, ironically, would be more at home at Harvard today than any of her critics."

The reason Founders Brook is called Founders Brook is because it marks the spot where, in 1638, Hutchinson's followers wrote and signed their mutual pledge that came to be known as the Portsmouth Compact. A plaque on another rock near the Women's Healing Garden and the little Hutchinson and Dyer memorials presents the compact's text:

We whose names are underwritten do here solemnly in the presence of Jehovah incorporate ourselves into a body politic and as he shall help, will submit our persons, lives and estates unto our lord Jesus Christ, the King of Kings, and Lord of Lords, and to all those perfect and most absolute laws of his given us in his Holy word of truth, to be guided and judged thereby.

The names of the compact's signers, including Anne Hutchinson's husband, Will, are listed below the text. Here lies the deepest reason why the Women's Healing Garden strikes me as so forlorn—that Hutchinson is remembered here by pink echinacea in bloom instead of on the Portsmouth Compact plaque, where she belongs. All of the signers were there because of her, because she stood up to Massachusetts and they stood with her. But all the signers were men. Anne Hutchinson wasn't allowed to sign the founding document of the colony she founded.

After Will's death in 1642, Anne Hutchinson moved with some of her children to the Dutch colony of New Netherland, near what is now the Split Rock Golf Course in the Bronx. In 1643, Anne and every member of her household, except one of her daughters, was killed by Indians at war with the Dutch.

Of course, John Winthrop is not particularly devastated by the loss; after all, he writes in his journal, "these people had cast off ordinances and churches."

Because New York's Hutchinson River is named after Anne Hutchinson, and a major highway is named after the river, the main road leading from New York City to Boston is called the Hutchinson River Parkway. My word, how Winthrop would cringe if he knew that. To get to his city, you see her name.

A few weeks prior to Anne Hutchinson's death, Winthrop notes in his journal that Roger Williams, passing through New Amsterdam to board a ship for England to secure a charter for Providence, had actually tried to negotiate a peace between the Dutch and their Indian opponents. Winthrop writes that thanks to Williams, peace was "reestablished between the Dutch and them." Alas for Hutchinson, that peace didn't stick.

It is during this 1643 voyage from New Amsterdam that Williams writes his Algonquian dictionary, *A Key to the Language of America*. It is an eventful trip. In London, Williams goes on a publishing binge, printing *A Key*, along with John Cotton's callous letter about his banishment, his response to Cotton's letter, and his diatribe on liberty of conscience, *The Bloudy Tenent*. He also secures a charter from Parliament for Providence, Newport, and Portsmouth. The three towns, the document claims,

have adventured to make a nearer neighborhood and society with the great body of the Narragansett, which may in time by the blessing of God upon their endeavors, lay a sure foundation of happiness to all America.

Among the names of parliamentarians signing the charter is one "H. Vane," the former governor of Massachusetts Bay.

Williams made another return visit to England in 1651, staying at Vane's house and hobnobbing with Puritan celebrities like Cromwell and the poet John Milton, author of *Paradise Lost* (whom Williams taught Hebrew in exchange for lessons in Dutch). But the person who would, some twelve years later, in 1663, make Williams's dream of codifying religious liberty come true was not one of his fellow Puritans. It was the philandering, theater-attending "merry monarch" of the Restoration himself, Charles II.

The new Rhode Island charter signed by the king proclaimed:

No person within the said colony, at any time hereafter shall be any wise molested, punished, disquieted, or called in question, for any differences in opinion in matters of religion, and do not actually disturb the civil peace of our said colony; but that all and every person and persons may, from time to time, and at all times hereafter, freely and fully have and enjoy his and their own judgments and consciences, in matters of religious concernments, throughout the tract of land hereafter mentioned, they behaving themselves peaceable and quietly.

While the previous charter had urged Rhode Island, like the Massachusetts Bay Charter of yore, to "conform to the laws of England," this one extends to the inhabitants of Rhode Island more freedom than the inhabitants of England.

In the years after Massachusetts forces Roger Williams, and then Anne Hutchinson, to trudge through the snow to Narragansett Bay, Williams's colony becomes a place of refuge for the unwanted and displaced, the outcasts and the cranks, including Baptists, Quakers, and Jews.

In *The Witches of Eastwick,* a novel set in a fictional, seemingly dull Rhode Island village, John Updike tips his hat to Rhode Island's weirdo founders. Satan moves to town and wonders why the alluring local witches live in such a humdrum place. "Tell him Narragansett Bay has always taken oddballs in," says one witch to another, "and what's he doing up here himself?"

That said, Williams's colony is hardly utopia. There is as much internecine squabbling—if not more—going on there as there is in Massachusetts.

In 1672, the sixty-nine-year-old Williams himself will wage a vicious war of words with the colony's Quakers because he believes they have "set up a false Christ." The Quaker belief in the "God within" each person is anathema to a Bible-based Calvinist like Williams, who writes in his screed against Quaker founder George Fox, *George Fox Digg'd Out of his Burrowes,* "they preached the Lord Jesus to be themselves."

Williams even holds a three-day-long debate in Newport with three Quakers. "The audience, mostly Baptists and Quakers," writes Perry Miller, "heckled him with cries of 'old man, old man,' and whispered, after he had on the first day shouted himself hoarse in order to get any hearing, that he was drunk." (More than three decades after John Cotton accused Williams of missing God's point back in Salem when he smote him with laryngitis, he was once again struck dumb during a spree of punditry.)

Here is the important difference between Massachusetts Bay and Narragansett Bay. Quakers such as Mary Dyer are hanged in Boston Common. In Rhode Island, there is bickering, but there is no banishing. There are mean-spirited spiritual debates, but no forced and freezing hikes of exile.

In 1675, Metacom, aka King Philip (the son of Williams's old Wampanoag friend Massasoit) assembled an army of allied native warriors, attacking English settlements across New England. In 1676, some of Philip's Narragansett allies burned down Providence. One English resident of the town believed the Word of God would protect him from the native invaders, who nevertheless "ripped him open, and put his Bible in his belly," according to one contemporary account. Williams's house went up in smoke, along with his lifelong sympathy for his Narragansett neighbors. After Philip's death—his head was displayed on a pike in Plymouth for the next twenty years—Williams was one of the colonial officials at the end of the war who approved the sale of vanquished Indians into slavery, primarily in Bermuda, where their descendants still reside.

Though Williams complained of being "old and weak and bruised" with "lameness on both my feet," he lived to see Providence rebuilt. He is well remembered there, having died in 1683 at the age of eighty. What was left of his remains was reburied in 1939 in a park on Prospect Terrace in which a colossal statue of Williams stares out across his city, giving him a view of the statue *Independent Man* on top of the Rhode Island State Capitol, where the Royal Charter of 1663 is, incidentally, housed.

One morning, I sat on a bench near the Williams statue eating breakfast, and from the open window of a passing car I heard rapper Eminem on the radio, asking, "May I have your attention, please?" as Williams must have asked so many times, trying to get the men and women of New England to hear what he had to say.

So Providence is an appropriate place to ponder Williams, but the best spot in Rhode Island to commune with his legacy is in the Touro Synagogue, in Newport. This fine colonial temple with its arches and columns is the oldest synagogue in the United States. The building was dedicated in 1763.

But the congregation dates back to 1658, when fifteen Jewish families sailed from the West Indies because they had heard of Roger Williams and his colony's commitment to freedom of worship.

In 1790, George Washington and Thomas Jefferson come to Newport, stumping for the Bill of Rights. (Rhode Island is the last state to ratify the Constitution precisely because its citizens hold out for a bill of rights so they can retain the freedom of religion they have enjoyed since the days of Roger Williams.) Moses Seixas, a member of the Touro Synagogue, wrote Washington a letter asking about his administration's policy toward Jews. Washington's response, addressed "to the Hebrew Congregation in Newport, Rhode Island," reassures Seixas and his brethren that the American government goes beyond mere tolerance:

The Citizens of the United States of America have a right to applaud themselves for having given to mankind examples of an enlarged and liberal policy: a policy worthy of imitation. All possess alike liberty of conscience and immunities of citizenship. It is now no more that toleration is spoken of, as if it was by the indulgence of one class of people, that another enjoyed the exercise of their inherent national gifts. For happily the Government of the United States . . . gives to bigotry no sanction, to persecution no assistance.

O ne hundred and seventy years after the first president wrote those words pledging freedom of religion in the United States, the thirty-fifth president was
elected. John Winthrop would have been delighted that the
new president came from a Boston family. That is, until
Winthrop learned that that Boston family was Catholic.

In a kind of microbial comeuppance, the Protestant bas-
tion Winthrop was able to build in the 1630s because a
plague had wiped out its original Indian inhabitants by 1620
would become the Catholic capital of America after an infectious mold destroyed the Irish potato crop in the 1840s,
flinging the refugees of the resulting famine, among them
the ancestors of John Fitzgerald Kennedy, to Boston in
droves, bringing their "popery" with them.

On January 9, 1961, eleven days before his inauguration,
President-elect Kennedy gives a speech at the State House
on Boston's Beacon Hill to a Joint Convention of the General Court of the Commonwealth of Massachusetts. His
opening remarks, including the fact that his grandparents
were born there and the hope that his grandchildren will be,
too, seem sentimental on the page. But in the sound record-
ing of that event, the tone of his voice is solemn, nearly fu-
nereal. He claims it is not a farewell address, but that is how
it sounds. He calls himself a "son of Massachusetts," and

here that does not come off as boosterism. To be a son of
Massachusetts is to carry the cumbersome weight of history,
though Kennedy is proud to bear that burden.

"For no man about to enter high office in this country
can ever be unmindful of the contributions which this state
has made to our national greatness," he tells them. "Its leaders have shaped our destiny long before the great republic
was born. For what Pericles said of the Athenians has long
been true of this commonwealth: 'We do not imitate—for
we are a model to others.'"

For a man who always looks so crisp and modern on film,
that last opinion could not be more antique. Nowadays, I
cannot imagine that an American president from Massachusetts would ever be allowed to stand up in his home state
and evoke Pericles in order to put forth the notion that the
rest of the country should look up to the place nicknamed
"Taxachusetts," the place where men are allowed to marry
other men. Nowadays, I cannot imagine an American from
Massachusetts could get elected president period, much
less a Harvard grad prone to elitist quotations from ancient
Greece.

Kennedy goes on to say,

The enduring qualities of Massachusetts—the common
threads woven by the Pilgrim and the Puritan, the fisher-
man and the farmer, the Yankee and the immigrant—will

not be and could not be forgotten in this nation's executive mansion.

"Allow me to illustrate," he says. He talks about how he's spent the last couple of months planning for his presidency. As he makes ready, one man has been on his mind.

"I have been guided by the standard John Winthrop set before his shipmates on the flagship *Arbella* three hundred and thirty-one years ago, as they, too, faced the task of building a new government on a perilous frontier," Kennedy says.

Then he boils down the two phrases from "A Model of Christian Charity" that mean the most to him: "We must always consider, [Winthrop] said, that we shall be as a city upon a hill. The eyes of all people are upon us."

I fall for those words every time I hear them, even though they're dangerous, even though they're arrogant, even though they're rude.

"Today the eyes of all people are truly upon us," Kennedy points out. He does not mention that the whole world is staring in America's direction because we have a lot of giant scary bombs, but I am guessing that is partly what he meant. He says that he hopes that all branches of government, from the top on down, are mindful of "their great responsibilities." Responsibilities that include trying not to use the giant scary bombs.

"For we are setting out upon a voyage in 1961 no less

hazardous than that undertaken by the *Arbella* in 1630," he continues. "We are committing ourselves to tasks of statecraft no less awesome than that of governing the Massachusetts Bay Colony, beset as it was by terror without and disorder within."

He then paraphrases the same verse from the Gospel of Luke that John Cotton evoked in 1630 in his farewell sermon to the passengers on the *Arbella*. "For of those to whom much is given, much is required." He says that history will judge him and everyone else on four things—courage, judgment, integrity, and dedication, "the historic qualities of the Bay Colony and the Bay State," Kennedy adds.

He does not sound entirely steady. "I ask for your help and your prayers, as I embark on this new and solemn journey," he pleads. At this grave moment, he is not a man merely talking about the *Arbella*. He is on the dock in Southampton, ready to board the *Arbella,* along with the people before him. The mood is ominous and the fear is real. But this is a new beginning and he is not alone.

MOST USEFUL PRIMARY SOURCES

The Complete Writings of Roger Williams, edited by Perry Miller, seven volumes (Russell & Russell, 1964; based on the Narragansett Club edition of 1867).

The Correspondence of Roger Williams, edited by Glenn W. La-Fantasie, two volumes (Rhode Island Historical Society/ Brown University Press, 1988).

John Cotton, "God's Promise to His Plantation" included in *The Puritans in America: A Narrative Anthology,* edited by Alan Heimert (Harvard University Press, 1985).

The Journal of John Winthrop, 1630–1649, edited by Richard S. Dunn, James Savage, and Laetitia Yeandle (Harvard University Press, 1996).

John Mason, *A Brief History of the Pequot War,* included in *Puritans in the New World: A Critical Anthology,* edited by David D. Hall (Princeton University Press, 2004).

The Puritans: A Sourcebook of Their Writings, edited by Perry Miller and Thomas H. Johnson (Dover, 2001; originally published by Harper & Row, 1963). Includes, among many others, William Bradford's *History of Plymouth Plantation,* Edward

Johnson's *Wonder-working Providence,* John Winthrop's "A Modell of Christian Charity," Thomas Hooker's "A True Night of Sin," Anne Bradstreet's poems, and Thomas Shephard, Jr.'s, letter to his son.

Roger Williams, *A Key into the Language of America* (Applewood Books, 1997; reprint of the fifth edition published by the Rhode Island and Providence Plantations Tercentenary Committee, 1936; originally published in London, 1643). *A Key* is included in *The Complete Writings of Roger Williams,* but this edition, issued by this heroic publisher, is especially handy and beautiful.

The Winthrop Papers, volumes 3, 4, and 5, edited by Allyn Bailey Forbes (Massachusetts Historical Society, 1943–47).

William Wood, *New England's Prospect* (University of Massachusetts Press, 1994; originally published in London, 1634).

John Underhill, *Newes from America* (University of Nebraska, 2007; originally published, 1638).

Note on Language

I have capitalized "God" throughout for two reasons—because the Protestants' deity is a character Himself, and as a way of constantly reminding the reader how present and powerful and terrifying this character was in the Puritans' lives. I have also slightly modernized some seventeenth-century spellings. There wasn't any uniform English spelling at the time, anyway. So when quoting letters and sermons, I have, for example, changed "humilitic" to "humility" and purged the superfluous "k" from the end of "Mystick" and the extra "l" from "modell" to make the text more uniform and easier on the reader. I have also gone with the spelling "Pequot" for that tribe, even though Winthrop and others called them "Pequod" (which is of course the spelling Herman Melville went with when naming Ahab's ship after them in *Moby-Dick*).

Acknowledgments

In the ten years he's been my editor and friend, Geoffrey Kloske has never let me down. The words "I'm so lucky" and "breathing down my neck" spring to mind.

Special thanks to: Amy Vowell and Owen Brooker for once again traveling with me to places they would prefer to avoid; David Levinthal for his cover photograph; Marcel Dzama for his illustration; Steven "the Colonel" Barclay and Sara Bixler at Steven Barclay Agency; Jaime Wolf for lawyering; Laura Perciasepe, Mih-Ho Cha, and copy editor Ed Cohen at Riverhead; Nick Hornby for his Englishness and kindness, though not necessarily in that order; David Shipley at the *New York Times* for editing an essay I cannibalized herein; Ira Glass for editing a *This American Life* essay I pilfered here as well, and for his many years of friendship, partnership, and editorial stewardship—all the best ships, really; my generous theological pen pal Reza Aslan; and always and particularly Bennett Miller for being Bennett Miller.

Also helpful and/or encouraging: J. J. Abrams; Brad Bird; Eric Bogosian; Michael Comeau and Jennifer Fauxsmith at the Massachusetts Archives; Patrick Daughters; Jeremy Dibbell and

Acknowledgments

Elaine Grublin at the Massachusetts Historical Society; Shelley Dick; Dave Eggers; Michael and Jamie Giacchino; Eric Gilliland; Jake Gyllenhaal; Daniel Handler; John Hodgman; Spike Jonze; Ben Karlin; Catherine Keener; Nick Laird; Lisa Leingang; Greil and Jenny Marcus; Tom McCarthy; Clyde, Dermot, Ellen, Kieran, and Michael Mulroney for their hospitality on Cape Cod; Jim Nelson; John Oliver; John Petrizzo; Christopher Quinn; David Rakoff; David Rosenthal; Rodney Rothman; David Sedaris; John-Mario Sevilla; Jonathan Marc Sherman; Zadie Smith; the Family Sontheimer; Pat and Janie Vowell for parenting; Gina Way; Wendy Weil; and Stu Zicherman.

This book is dedicated to Scott Seeley, Ted Thompson, and Joan Kim, the founding staff of 826NYC in Brooklyn. They share a reverence for words and the ideal of community with the Massachusetts Bay Colony (but not the banishing or the burning people alive). Thanks to them, the city on the hill might be Park Slope.

Sarah Vowell is an American original. With her wit, wisdom, and unerring sense of history, politics, and humor, she tells stories of our country's past—the good, the bad, and the ugly. In her inimitable, wry style, history has never been so troubling, so alive, or so funny.

"Sarah Vowell is a Madonna of Americana."

—*Los Angeles Times*

"I love Sarah Vowell's writing—it's smart, funny, soulful, even educational." —**Nick Hornby**

"Vowell makes an excellent traveling companion, what with her rare combination of erudition and cheek."

—Bruce Handy, *The New York Times Book Review*

by Bennett Miller

Featuring a cast of beguiling, appalling, and tragic characters, including sugar barons, con men, brother-husbands, Theodore Roosevelt, and the last Hawaiian queen...

Sarah Vowell explores the Americanization of Hawaii—from the arrival of New England missionaries in 1820 to the events leading up to American annexation in 1898.

With her wry insights and reporting, Vowell explores the odd, emblematic, and exceptional history of the fiftieth state and, in so doing, finds America, warts and all.

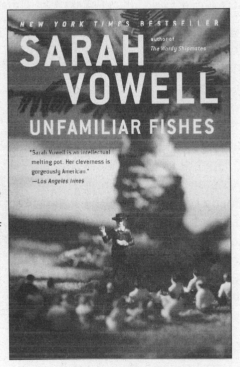

NEW YORK TIMES BESTSELLER

author of
The Wordy Shipmates

SARAH VOWELL

UNFAMILIAR FISHES

"Sarah Vowell is an intellectual melting pot. Her cleverness is gorgeously American."
—Los Angeles Times

"A tour de force...Vowell is a national treasure, exploring the depths of what it means to be American." **—The Boston Globe**

"Sarah Vowell is an intellectual melting pot. Her cleverness is gorgeously American." **—Los Angeles Times**

From the bestselling author of *Assassination Vacation* and *The Partly Cloudy Patriot*, an insightful and unconventional account of George Washington's trusted officer and friend, that swashbuckling teenage French aristocrat the Marquis de Lafayette.

Chronicling General Lafayette's years in Washington's army, Vowell reflects on the ideals of the American Revolution versus the reality of the Revolutionary War. Riding shotgun with Lafayette, Vowell swerves from the high-minded debates of Independence Hall to the frozen wasteland of Valley Forge, from bloody battlefields to the Palace of Versailles, bumping into John Adams, Thomas Jefferson, Lord Cornwallis, Benjamin Franklin, Marie Antoinette, and various kings, Quakers, and redcoats along the way.

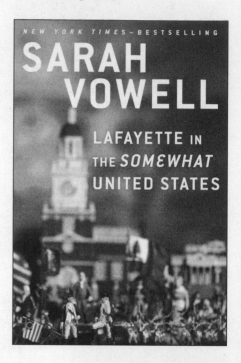

"[A] freewheeling history of the Revolutionary War." —*The New Yorker*

"Vowell wanders through the history of the American Revolution and its immediate aftermath, using Lafayette's involvement in the war as a map, and bringing us all along in her perambulations....Her prose sparkles." —*The New York Times Book Review*

"Gilded with snark, buoyant on charm, Vowell's brand of history categorically refuses to take itself—or any of its subjects—too seriously." —**NPR**